BECOMING DAD

A True Story of One Man's Transformation

from Clueless Husband to Involved and

Nurturing Father

KELLY CRULL

concha
books

CONCHA BOOKS
Bilingual Books in English and Spanish for Kids and Parents
www.conchabooks.com
info@conchabooks.com
+1 (605) 610-0231 (USA)
+34 644 39 50 08 (Spain)

First Paperback Edition

ISBN-13: 978-84-615-5068-5

Cover design by Gloria Byler
Author photograph © Kelly Crull

for Alleke

CONTENTS

Pregnancy

Baby

Toddler

ACKNOWLEDGEMENTS

When I casually mentioned to my wife that I had decided to dedicate this book to our daughter, she said, "So I get nothing?"

So, first of all, I would like to thank my wife, April, for her companionship. I lost track of how many times she rearranged her schedule so I could write while she watched the kids. She listened to me talk about writing and publishing on countless date nights. She read drafts and made edits on her days off. And, she still thought this book was worth writing.

Thanks to Kim Boer, Marlies De Jeu, Bridget De Yager, Katrina Geertsma, Lindsay Hilkert, Julie Lemley, Kim Ray, and Gwyneth Box for their edits.

Thanks to my friends at the Madrid Writers Critique Group, especially Sue Burke, Sean McLachlan and Lance Tooks.

Thanks to family and friends for providing me with healthy examples of family, in particular my parents, Steve and Pat, who always made time for me, my sister Monica and her husband Jeff who let me live with them during the pregnancy and birth of my niece Josie, Byron and Lisa Borden for their wisdom, and Dan and Diane Ridderhoff for letting me live with them one summer in high school. I had honestly never considered the possibility of a stay-at-home dad until I met Dan.

Thanks to my mother-in-law, Rachel, my sister-in-law, Heidi, Laurie Schmitt, the Cadys, Bowles, and Repettos, Kelly Jennemann, Shani Kilasi, Amy Swacina, our midwife Carmen, Damián and Encarna, Jitu Dongardive, and Adriana Cardona, who shaped this story. Thanks to God for the gift of new life and trusting me to care for a few of his little ones.

PART I

Pregnancy

Pregnancy Test

"Do you want me to run down to the pharmacy and get another one?" I asked.

April shrugged. She sat down on the edge of the tub and looked out the window for a while, then buried her face in her hands and wept, her shoulders shaking.

I didn't know for sure if we were pregnant. Could we trust this piece of plastic? It was disposable, but I was supposed to believe the results were permanent, irreversible, eternal?

Still, that punch-in-the-gut feeling was not doubt, but certainty. April was crying at the edge of the tub because pregnancy was no longer a concept, but a reality.

Five weeks earlier we had visited some friends with a house on the beach. Their two-month-old Tiffany was dangerously cute. She was a fat little cherub without wings. For the first time having a baby didn't sound like the worst idea, and so, we simply decided to stop not getting pregnant. After all, everyone said getting pregnant could take years. We agreed that we wanted a baby, but we were far from imagining a child in our future.

We had been married for six years, and all that time people had been asking us when we would start a family. I began to believe we were late. Until today, that is, when we took the pregnancy test and all of a sudden we had no choice but to look at the world from a new point of view. I felt young again, but not in a good way. I was horrified at what we had done. I felt guilt and shame and irresponsibility like I was a teenage boy who had knocked up his girlfriend. My stomach swarmed like a beehive. "What are we going to do with a baby?" I thought.

We were not ready for a baby. We had recently moved to Castellón, a small village in Spain where we had no friends, which was no surprise since we were still relying mostly on our high school Spanish. April was in the middle of a Master's degree in Peace and Development Studies, and I was not making enough money working from home as a web designer to pay our bills.

Maybe I had deliberately avoided preparing myself mentally for having a baby. I knew I would only be able to handle this pregnancy one step at a time. At first I was ready to try to get pregnant, and that was enough. Now that we were pregnant, I needed time to let go of the life I had, everything that was familiar and basic to me, for something unpredictable and even unnecessary. Most likely April and I wouldn't go to Spanish class together or go to the movies together or even get groceries together. We would travel less, go out with friends less, and have sex less. The list streamed through my brain like headlines at the bottom of a television screen. I suppose there was never a good time to have a baby because it would always mean trading in the life I already had for one I didn't know anything about.

I would no longer be the same person, April would no longer be the same person, and now we had everything to learn about the newest addition to our family.

8 WEEKS, 1 DAY
Doctor's Visit

"Wait. Is this where we're going?" I asked. I came to a complete stop on the sidewalk.

"Right here," April said. "Come on, we're late."

I didn't move.

"You didn't say we were going to the gynecologist," I said and nodded at the sign over the front door.

April sighed and put her hands on her hips. "Where else do you think a woman goes for a pregnancy checkup?"

Without waiting for an answer, she turned and walked into

the clinic. I frowned, shook my head, and reluctantly followed her inside as if I had just been asked to follow her into the women's bathroom.

April signed in, and the nurse pointed the way to the waiting room where a small crowd of women glanced at us from behind their women's magazines. My worst fear had been confirmed: I was the only man in this clinic. We took the last two seats in the room, and I felt like I was having one of those dreams where I was in a public place like the grocery store and happened to catch a glimpse of myself in a mirror only to realize I was naked. Frankly, I would not have felt less awkward sitting in that waiting room completely naked. Not that the women would have noticed. They were absorbed in their magazines.

The tingling in my fingers, my heart pulsing in my chest like an electric fence, feeling warm all over, shortness of breath, I recognized the symptoms. I was embarrassed. The feeling reminded me of being sent to the store to buy tampons for my wife or being convinced to wait in the women's lingerie section by myself while April tried on a sweater. I wasn't worried that someone we knew might see us and know our secret. After all, we only knew a handful of students at the university. I felt embarrassed because everyone in the waiting room knew the only reason a guy goes to the gynecologist is because there's a good chance the girl sitting next to him is pregnant.

I was making my debut as an expectant father, and now that I was here, I knew I wasn't ready to have an audience. I hadn't dared to think of myself as a father yet. In fact, if I had applied for the job—if that's how becoming a dad worked—I would not have been called in for an interview. I was young and unqualified with little to no experience. My own mother had told me I was "not particularly good with kids," as if it was common knowledge. I wanted to be a dad, but I wasn't one yet.

Meanwhile, April eyed the magazines on the coffee table until she found one she liked. She picked it up, opened it, and began to read.

8 WEEKS, 1 DAY
Ultrasound

A few minutes later April was reclined on a hospital bed, and I was sitting in a chair next to her holding her hand. Both of us were watching over our doctor's shoulder as she clicked around the screen, took measurements of our little tadpole and dictated them to her assistant.

I was surprised. Not to see the baby, and not that the baby looked like a tadpole, but because I felt like something was missing.

Although I didn't think of myself as a father yet, the truth was I wanted to feel like one. That's why I was here. For a moment, it made more sense to imagine us in Bern, Switzerland where April was reclined on a sofa covered with elaborate tapestries and lots of pillows, I was sitting in a chair next to her holding her hand, and Hermann Rorschach, the great Swiss psychiatrist, was at his desk. He reached over and handed me one of his famous flash cards.

"What do you see on the card?" he asked. "How does the card make you feel?"

I stared blankly at the card.

"I see a tadpole," I said. "I don't *feel* anything."

I was looking for more than a tadpole on a flash card. I was waiting for something to kick in. I didn't know exactly what, but something very instinctive and paternal that would set into motion my great metamorphosis into the dad I would become. I expected to be changed by seeing this little person. I was counting on it, but nothing happened. I felt the same, like I was watching a meteorologist explain weather patterns on Doppler radar.

"This isn't working," I said. I looked at the card again and shook my head.

Rorschach leaned back in his chair for a moment, stroked his mustache, and then he looked me in the eyes.

"Most of the time we don't choose the important moments in our lives," he said. "The important moments choose us." He paused. "What matters is that we embrace these moments when they come along."

Rorschach was right. I didn't feel like a dad, but that didn't matter. I couldn't wait around for instinct to kick in. I wasn't the pregnant one after all. Unlike April whose hormones were literally transforming her into a fully-functional baby-care facility complete with heated Jacuzzi and all-you-can-eat buffet, becoming a dad was a choice—less instinct, like grabbing a snack when I felt hungry, and more choice, like making myself get out of bed in the morning to go for a run.

I didn't feel different. I didn't look different. But I was choosing to be a dad.

9 WEEKS
Sailing

Calling family and friends to tell them we're pregnant has begun to feel like telemarketing. I spend weekends on the phone with a list of people to call and a script of what to say when they pick up. Maybe I should end the conversation by asking them if they would like to consolidate their student loans.

Because no one in Castellón knows we're pregnant yet, I only feel like we're pregnant when I'm on the telephone, like I'm somebody who dresses up in chain mail on the weekends and goes to medieval festivals.

I'm no good at keeping secrets either. The only way I've managed to keep my mouth shut when I'm not on the phone is to try to forget we're pregnant altogether, which seems counter productive since in reality I need all the help I can get to believe we are actually pregnant.

So, April and I agreed to tell one person in Castellón. We chose Laurie, even though she is not family, and we have only known her for five months. Laurie is a mother, and if anyone would know how to make the pregnancy seem real, she would. Plus, she lives around the corner and sees April every day at class. No doubt she would remind us we were pregnant.

We met at a hot dot stand, and I don't think Laurie noticed we weren't eating our hot dogs. We were concentrated on watching her squeeze mustard on her hot dog when April broke the silence.

"We have something to tell you."

Laurie looked at both of us, then set down the mustard.

"We're pregnant," April said.

Laurie's face twisted into a pained expression, as if these very words had welled up inside of her a storm of emotions so unexpected and so fierce she could not brace herself in time.

We sat with our hot dogs and watched her giggle while she wiped tears from her eyes.

Watching a friend cry is not easy. I wanted to say something, but I didn't because I didn't know why she was crying. I knew she was crying because we were pregnant, but she also seemed to be crying as a mother, as someone who knew more than we did. She cried like someone watching the opera, or like someone reminded of a story that needed to be told.

I felt the winds begin to blow. Our sails bellied, and we were finally moving, gliding across the water, as if Laurie's tears had somehow launched us on our journey. We were no longer harbored in the life we had known up to this point, but sailing into the storm.

We needed Laurie, now more than ever. Not to remind us that this was real, which seemed obvious now, but to show us the way forward.

9 WEEKS, 3 DAYS
Naps

I unlocked the door with one hand, rolled my bike into the apartment with the other, and after a flutter of helmet, keys, shoes and sweatshirt, found the place completely quiet.

"Hello?"

No answer.

"April?"

Still no answer.

I walked to the office where April's desk was. No April. I put my head in the kitchen. No April. I checked the den. No April.

I walked back through the apartment to our bedroom and opened the door. The covers lumped together around what I could only guess was a human-sized kidney bean. Without a sound, I sat on the side of the bed and rubbed the covers over April's back. Slowly she came to life, wriggling a bit, then turning over and pulling the covers down over her chin. She rubbed her eyes.

"What?" she asked. She squinted at me and then at the alarm clock. She pulled the covers back over her head.

I couldn't help it. I laughed.

"It's okay if you take naps," I said. "You're pregnant."

She pulled the covers down below her eyes and looked at me suspiciously.

"But I have to write my paper," she said. I swear she was pouting.

"It's okay if you take a nap." I repeated myself, realizing then that these words were becoming a daily mantra.

She took a deep breath, sighed, and stared angrily at the ceiling. I kissed her on the cheek, then leaned across the bed and turned off the alarm clock.

"I'll check on you later," I whispered. I left the bedroom and closed the door behind me.

10 WEEKS, 5 DAYS
Baby Food

No, I'm not referring to the goo that comes in jars. I'm sure there will be time to experiment with that later. I'm talking about the food my pregnant wife demands for the baby before the baby is even born. What she eats, the baby eats.

April's requests are a royal decree. "In the name of our baby, The Royal Highness," April says, "I request Stuffed Eggplant for dinner."

Who can argue with an embryo?

April even sent me a link this morning to the recipe she had in mind. I thought she was busy studying at the university library, but it turns out she was looking up stuffed eggplant recipes. I had no idea a baby in the womb could have so much control over how we spend our time.

Two hours later, no exaggeration, and I had dinner on the table.

A banquet fit for royalty.

11 WEEKS, 1 DAY
Pesto

A plate of warm pasta. The elegance of extra-virgin olive oil. The vitality of basil. The adventure of garlic. The nuance of pine nuts. And oh, bittersweet Parmesan sprinkled on top.

This is pesto.

Who says women are the only ones who have pregnancy cravings? I am living proof that men do too.

It's not difficult to find out what men crave when their wives are pregnant. They crave every food their wives stopped eating when they got pregnant.

I saw April get sick. I heard how she bad-mouthed her favorite foods. There's no way I'm going to eat those foods in front of her. Still, secretly, I crave them.

Tonight April's out. She won't be back for dinner. As I write these final words, the pasta is boiling on the stove, an open bottle of wine is sitting on the table, and that one special jar of my favorite pesto sauce is waiting for me at the back of the kitchen cupboard.

13 WEEKS, 5 DAYS
Pregnancy Brain

Sunday we had lunch with our landlords, Damián and Encarna. We sat around the table outside next to the pool while Encarna brought out the food from the kitchen. April looked so tired, I thought she might curl up in the shade of one of their lemon trees and go to sleep. April was so worn out, in fact, she couldn't keep her Spanish straight. She was beyond being frustrated. She was too tired to care, so she kept talking anyway, which was like listening to a drunk tell a story.

I wanted to say, "April's okay, really. She's got pregnancy brain. She'll just keep getting slower and more forgetful every day until the baby is born. It's an amazing phenomenon to watch, actually."

But I had better judgment.

This is all part of a longer story about learning languages. April and I have always learned languages together, even in high school. In almost every regard, we speak at the same level.

However, we have our differences. Without a doubt I try harder. I read books in Spanish. I rehearse Spanish conversations while I make dinner. I have a weekly language exchange with a guy named Marcos.

Still, April learns as much as I do. I suppose you could say April pays closer attention to details, but when it comes down to it, I think April just has better hardware than I do.

She's smart.

I remember one day having tea with our host mom in Amsterdam while April and I were studying abroad and learning Dutch. She looked at April and said, "You've learned Dutch very quickly. You must have a knack for languages." I was feeling pretty good about our improvement until I realized she wasn't talking to me. "Kelly, you struggle," she said. Much less inspired by this thought, she moved on to the next topic of conversation.

So, you see, I've been patiently waiting my turn. I realize taking advantage of my pregnant wife is not nice, especially when she feels dumber every day, reading articles like "The Subsistence Perspective: Beyond the Globalised Economy" or "An Introduction to Development and the Anthropology of Modernity."

Still, seeing pregnancy is a temporary thing, I can't see how it will hurt anyone if I enjoy a brief moment of intellectual superiority.

Seems smart to me, don't you think?

16 WEEKS
Boy or Girl?

"Actually, I can't tell," the doctor said. She took both her hands and pressed gently on April's firm stomach. The baby on the screen wiggled, even yawned, and settled back into a comfortable position.

The doctor scratched her face and looked at the screen.

The baby was resting comfortably. Wombs are apparently a good place for a nap.

We watched the screen as the ultrasound image outlined the spinal column, in perfect form, ten fingers, ten toes, even the stomach, an empty hole, and the heart, all chambers throbbing.

We could see the baby inside and out.

Still, the doctor shook her head.

"I can't tell," she said again, admitting defeat.

Sure enough. We looked at the screen, and there was the baby—legs crossed modestly. There was no way to tell if this little baby was a boy or girl unless he or she decided to change napping positions.

I smiled. Already our baby was making decisions. The baby had decided to cross his or her legs, and there was nothing we could do about it.

"We can wait," I said. I looked away from the screen towards the doctor. "Maybe the baby's not ready for us to know."

18 WEEKS, 1 DAY
Carrefour

I'll admit it—I freaked out a little on Tuesday night when April and I were tossing around ideas about how we would spend our date night.

We had been busy the last two weeks with April finishing her Masters classes and me meeting a hefty deadline at work. My parents would arrive on Wednesday to stay for three weeks, so Tuesday night was our night, our chance to be together just the two of us.

I suggested we go for dinner at Tasca Dos, a little restaurant with tables that spilled out into the plaza, followed by a chilled-out night at home—maybe we would watch a movie or an episode of *Lost*.

When it was April's turn, she said she wanted to go shopping at Carrefour, a large French department store. We needed a few things before we went on vacation with my parents to Germany next week, like a new carry-on suitcase and some socks and underwear, and now was really the best time to go since we were booked the rest of the week.

I got grumpy. I told April we were getting old. I reminded her that we were already parents, and there was nothing we could do about that now. Any romance we had once had in our relationship was already being replaced by the practicalities of parenthood. I thought of the baby things cluttering our bedroom.

It's not that I don't want to have a baby. Believe me, when I was at the beach today, and I saw all those little kids splashing around in the water, I wanted one of my own.

But what scares me more than anything else about having a little person in our lives is not having enough time for everyone, including April and me.

Time is the best gift. I love being with April, even if we're just sitting on the couch with our laptops, even if she's writing a paper in the living room and I'm coding a website for a client in the office.

I want to be able to give time to our little one, to April and to myself, but it feels like I'm full already. I'm stuffed with life. I can't eat another bite. I'm obese. I need to go on a time diet.

In the end, I told April I'd be good. We went to Carrefour, and we bought a suitcase and socks and underwear. We made the best of the night, walking hand-in-hand to the store and talking all the way.

I guess that's the lesson learned. Time is time, and you might as well make the best of it—whether you're eating a romantic dinner at Tasca Dos or standing in line at the checkout at Carrefour.

On Call

For weeks I had been pedaling across town on my bike trying not to consider what an accurate metaphor this bicycle was for my own physical condition. We talked like a master and his aging dog.

"Come on, boy," I'd say, "you can make it."

He (the bike) would begin whimpering the moment we left the front door of our apartment building, yelping occasionally as he heaved himself one paw after another over each curb and pothole. Getting to class on time was like dragging him on a leash the entire way.

I must have been inspired by the tales of my friend Andy, the veterinarian, who visited last week because here I was in the kitchen doing a major operation on my bike, which rested upside-down on the floor.

I sloshed water over the frame. I hammered chunks of fossilized dirt from the gears with a screwdriver. I even discovered an abandoned bottle of WD-40 in my toolbox and perfumed the air with the smell of my dad's workshop as the spray washed away rust and grime. I turned one of the pedals with my hand and the rear wheel began to spin. I turned faster and faster, the sounds from the kinks in the back tire steadying into a rhythm that hummed like a washing machine.

We had a heartbeat—for a few moments, at least—before things turned for the worse. Turning the pedal with one hand, I began clicking through the gears with the other. The bike convulsed as the chain coughed and choked from one gear to the next before howling so loudly I thought we were going into cardiac arrest. I had four more gears to go, and the bike wouldn't budge. He was flatlining.

I was hoping it wouldn't come to this, but I was prepared to do anything. I would even consult the user's manual. While the bike lay motionless on the floor in the middle of the kitchen, I read through the section on "Adjustment of the Right Shift lever/Rear derailleur" and meticulously followed each step of the procedure.

Nearly an hour and a half had passed on the operating table all leading up to this moment. With only a few turns of the gears I would know whether I had saved a life or lost a faithful companion. What was done was done. I was ready.

I gripped the pedal with my right hand.

"Kelly? Are you in the kitchen?"

April was calling me from the living room, but I felt like she was calling me from another place completely, another story, in fact.

"Yeah," I said, "I'm in the kitchen," my hand still on the pedal.

"Come here a second," she said. "The baby just moved, and I can feel it with my hand."

This was our new game. The baby moves, and I come running. So far, I hadn't made it in time. I wasn't fast enough.

Feeling the baby move was like a fire drill—drop everything and exit the building immediately. I didn't expect that. I guess I didn't think the baby would interrupt what I was doing so much, at least while he or she was corralled in mama's playpen. I thought the baby would fit into the cracks, into my spare time, when I wasn't busy.

Of course I knew our lifestyle would have to change later. I've watched my sister carry her kids at arms' length to the bathroom for a diaper change. I've talked with plenty of parents who think it's the most natural thing in the world to carry on a conversation and holler at your kids at the same time.

Maybe being more flexible was something I needed to learn for now too. If I was going to feel the baby move, I needed to be on call. I had to be less like a surgeon and more like a paramedic.

I took my hand from the pedal and looked at it. It was gloved with oil. My socks soaked in a puddle of muddy water. Clods of dirt smeared the floor. Tools littered the room. I looked around for something to wipe off my hands.

At least for now, I wasn't going anywhere.

20 WEEKS, 3 DAYS
Ways to Show Affection

I subscribe to *The Sun Magazine*, and recently I read an essay called "Ways to Show Affection." The essay is by a woman named Virginia Eliot who writes about her experience sitting in an abortion clinic contemplating her second abortion. She pulls apart a tangled mess of story and leaves the reader as haunted as she is by her own obsession with being pregnant and the reality of being a mother.

She recounts the experience of being pregnant subjectively and completely—the cocooning of her body, the self-absorption of a new mother, the habit of studying other parents with their children, and the devotion of a mother to her unborn child. She writes:

> Pregnancy is a lot like hunger. It sits at the bottom of your stomach and controls your every thought. You try to distract yourself from it, but nothing works for long. Children on the street look like fresh-baked bread; babies in their mother's arms, the sweetest pastries. You stop and stare, and the back of your throat gets hot with desire. You lie in bed at night and think of suckling infants when you touch yourself.

Virginia's essay caught me on a day when having a baby felt less like the miracle of new life and more like a long to-do list:

- Research baby carriers online.
- Make a list of questions to ask our doctor at next checkup.
- Try to keep upcoming baby shower a secret from April. Sssshhh!
- Sign up for childbirth classes.
- Call the midwife who was recommended to us.
- Take a tour of the hospital.
- Call dentist to make an appointment for April. (Pregnancy is hard on teeth.)
- Make a list of baby names I like.

I asked April for suggestions to put on this list, and as I'm writing these words, she's still listing off things we need to do. In other words, the list goes on.

In the same way that hospitals can sometimes seem over-medicalized for an event that continues to happen naturally in many parts of the world—my friend Jitu from India tells me that in some parts of his country women deliver their own babies while they're at work in the fields—I don't like the thought that we may be burying ourselves in too many logistical details to see the miracle happening right here in our own home.

I don't want to take for granted the safe, healthy baby we have growing in April's belly.

Yesterday helped me remember why I want to be a dad. Our friends Troy and Heather are visiting from Madrid, and I got to make a sand castle with their son Nic who is six. I realize April and I aren't going to have a six-year old around for a while, but I enjoyed playing in the sand. Nic and I scooped out a moat around the castle, filled the moat with sea water from a plastic pale, and watched the water seep into the sand. Afterwards, I helped Nic pile sand over his dad until all we could see of him was his sunburned face.

Come to think of it, I can't wait to be a dad.

P.S. Virginia, thanks for your essay. I hope someday you'll find yourself looking into the eyes of your own child.

20 WEEKS, 5 DAYS
Spoiler

"She looks healthy," the doctor said while she drew circles on the frozen ultrasound image with a trackball and typed things into the computer.

April and I looked at each other.

"Sorry, what did you say?" I asked.

"I said she looks healthy," the doctor said, looking at us over her shoulder and nodding at the ultrasound.

"The baby's a girl?" April asked.

The doctor stopped typing and stared at the ultrasound.

"Most definitely."

She swiveled around in her chair and looked at us.

"I didn't tell you the sex of the baby at the last appointment?"

We shook our heads. "No, you couldn't tell because the baby's legs were crossed," I said. "I mean *her* legs were crossed," I added, correcting myself.

The doctor scratched her face and looked at the screen again.

"Well, you have a baby girl," she said, and shrugged.

22 WEEKS, 5 DAYS
Belly

This past weekend we were in Madrid. We got on the metro Friday night, and there was nowhere to sit. The car was packed. A man sitting in the back corner looked at April, then got up and stood next to the door.

April looked at me and grinned. "He just gave me his seat because I'm pregnant," she said, gloating. She walked over and sat down.

This is the third incident of its kind. There was the guy in Castellón, the first one, who reverently gave April his seat at mass. Then there was the waiter at the restaurant who offered wine to everyone but April. And now this guy on the metro.

It was official. April was showing.

The funny thing was April and I couldn't tell. We had no idea. All this time I was hoping April would get really big—simply because I thought it would be cool, which April thought was just plain mean. In the end, I couldn't even tell the difference because I was with April too often to notice the gradual changes happening to her body.

Over all, though, I am incredibly thankful that becoming a parent is a gradual process. If storks really did drop babies in blankets on our doorsteps, I would need at least nine months to prepare anyway.

When I think of all the things we still have to do in order to have the baby, like the fact that we still haven't chosen a name, I have to remind myself to take it one day at a time. If I do a little bit today, and a little bit tomorrow, and a little bit the day after that, it all adds up to a lot of little bits.

Maybe I can't always see the progress we were making, but if the guy on the metro can, I suppose that counts for something.

23 WEEKS, 2 DAYS
Evolution

The phone rang. I reached over April and fumbled for the phone from the nightstand.

"Hello?"

"Hey, it's Mimi."

She hesitated. "Are you in bed already?"

I looked at the clock. "Um..."

"Oh, I'm so sorry. I woke you up. Never mind then."

"No, it's okay," I said, sitting up in bed. "I was..." I spotted my book on the nightstand. "I was just reading in bed and dozed off," I said.

"Oh," she said, sounding confused. "Well, in that case, we're around the corner at the green place getting cocktails. Do you want to come down for a drink?"

I glance at the clock again, then at April sound asleep, her hand resting on her belly.

"I'll be there in five minutes," I said.

The second floor of the bar seemed to be reserved for close friends, a living room of sorts, scattered with old furniture, the kind you would find left at the dumpster on a college campus at the end of the semester. The waiter, who appeared be a drinking buddy when he wasn't working, sat on the arm of the couch next to me, discussing plans for the weekend and anticipating everyone's order until he got to me.

I gave up on the drinks menu and ordered a mojito. A familiar drink might help me shake the feeling that my friends had invited me out for a drink because they knew I didn't get out much now that April was pregnant, and they felt sorry for me.

Once the waiter left, Mimi leaned over and whispered in my ear what everyone else in the room was probably already thinking, "The mojitos aren't very good here. We get them at this other place. We'll take you sometime."

I forced a smile.

The waiter brought my drink. I sat and watched the mint leaves float at the top of the glass. It was turning out to be one of those nights when going out for a cocktail seemed like brainwashing. Who thought it was a good idea to have a drink in a sweaty bar with worn-out furniture where you couldn't hear what anyone was saying and you would spend upwards of nine euros for a glass of mostly crushed ice and fizzy water?

The coffee table in front of me was littered with empty glasses. My friends lounged on their sofas having conversations—making it work somehow.

The fish out of water feeling was what made me realize at that moment that I had evolved. My friends were right. I was not the person I used to be, even three months before. I had no social life anymore, and regardless of that fact, I still didn't want to be at this bar.

Why do people stop doing things they love so much when they have kids? The answer seemed obvious to me now. They find something they love to do even more. It wasn't so much that I didn't like going out for drinks anymore, but that I would rather be home with April.

I suppose the evolutionary process started with going to bed early with April when she got pregnant. We've always gone to bed together, so I didn't think much about going to bed early. The change in bedtime, however, meant that we had less time together in the evenings, so I made it a priority to be home most nights. While I was home, I discovered that making a baby takes all nine months. It's a hobby in its own right. If I wasn't making dinner for April, or we weren't tackling the next conversation on our pregnancy to-do list, I was sitting next to her on the couch running my fingers through her hair while she cried again for no apparent reason.

I hadn't intended to become someone else. I had simply prioritized.

I left my drink on the arm of the sofa. I paid the waiter and waved to Mimi before bounding down the steps into the street.

I started walking. I knew exactly where I wanted to be.

Encarna

I can't believe I'm saying this, but every month I look forward to paying our water and electric bills. The reason I don't mind paying the bills is because it gives me an excuse to visit Encarna in her antique shop.

I realized very soon after April got pregnant that Encarna is always on the lookout for more grandchildren. She collects them like she collects antiques. From the time Encarna greets me at the door of her shop to the time I finally find the courage to leave the envelope with her, we only talk about one thing—the baby. I love it.

This last time I went for a visit I scribbled a few baby names on a sticky-note and pasted it on the front of the envelope. April and I wanted to know what a few of our baby names sounded like in Spanish, so I was hoping to run them by Encarna since she doesn't speak English and would pronounce the names in Spanish.

Encarna took one look at the names and said, "I think you should name her Abril, after her mother." Abril is the Spanish version of April. That name was not on the list.

Regardless, Encarna had made up her mind, and she proceeded to walk through her store asking her customers if they didn't think Abril was the most beautiful name for my daughter.

Many of the customers looked confused, so she took the time to explain the whole scenario, who I was, that my wife was pregnant with a little girl, and that she thought our little girl's name should be Abril.

One of the women said, "I like Ana."

Encarna smiled politely and tried again.

"No," Encarna continued, "I said Abril. Don't you think

Abril is the most beautiful name for his daughter?" She wasn't asking the question as much as telling the woman what she was supposed to say.

"Oh, yes, Abril," the woman said. "It's beautiful."

Encarna was persistent until finally she had filled my sticky-note with a tally of votes for the name Abril, the most beautiful name for our daughter.

Pseudo-Grandma had cast her vote, and she had rallied the townspeople behind her.

25 WEEKS, 5 DAYS

Lunch

Most of my friends back home don't believe me when I tell them little children play in the streets in Spain after midnight. Most nights during the summer I fall asleep with the windows open and the sound of children playing in the square six stories below.

April and I worked in Madrid for three years before moving to Castellón for April's studies. Many of the international families we knew in Madrid didn't think twice about sending their kids to bed at eight o'clock, even if their kids sat pouting at the window watching their friends scream bloody murder in the playground below.

Still, sending kids to bed "early" in Spain gets complicated. My friend Jesús says his mom had dinner on the table every night at 10:15. That's over two hours after my international friends have tucked in their little ones. So, if I choose to put my kids to bed early because I think they need more sleep, I choose to either a) eat with my kids but not at the Spanish meal time, so putting myself further outside of the culture or b) eat my dinner after the kids are in bed, and so sacrifice having dinner together regularly as a family, which is something that's important to me.

I was telling Laurie my thoughts because Laurie's an incredible listener. Last week at dinner she listened to me talk about coding web pages in PHP for at least half an hour, and the entire time she smiled and asked questions and pretended to be interested.

When I finished explaining that I wanted to find a way to put my kids to bed early but also eat meals with them, Laurie sat quietly, thinking, then asked me, "When you were growing up, did you eat lunch with your parents?"

I thought for a moment. "No," I said, "I was at school."

Laurie pondered my answer.

When Laurie's not solving my problems, she's teaching history in international schools around the world. She's such a good teacher by now that often all she has to do is ask one question, and I've already learned something.

"Actually," I said, "I didn't eat breakfast with my parents either, at least not my dad. He left for work before I was out of bed."

I was in fact answering my own question. Without realizing it, I had stamped "Extra Important" on having the evening meal together as a family because in my family that's what we did. I hadn't considered that we rarely ate breakfast or lunch together.

In Spain, the most important meal of the day is lunch. Often Mom and Dad and the kids have a couple hours off to go home for lunch. Of course times are changing and sometimes kids stay at school while Mom and Dad eat lunch out with their colleagues, but I think many families still have lunch together.

Perhaps having lunch together every day was an idea. April and I could have lunch with our kids and put them to bed on time.

It's funny how sometimes I have these ideas in my head about what's important, and I don't even realize it. I can't think outside of those structures. I've always imagined eating dinner with my kids and having family time in the evening. Family time over lunch didn't cross my mind.

I'm sure life will only get busier with a little girl in our lives. I don't really care what time of day I get to be with her, as long as I get to be with her sometimes.

Beach Ball

We took the bus to the beach this afternoon. I set the backpack down in the sand, unzipped it, and began emptying the contents out around me—frisbee, sun tan lotion, books, towels.

April sat down on her knees in the sand and dug a small hole. When she finished the hole was about the size of a beach ball.

She carefully unrolled the green beach towel and draped it over the hole. She smoothed out the corners of the towel, then pressed the towel into the hole.

April picked up her book and lay down on the towel, burrowing her belly into the hole in the sand with the dignity and satisfaction of a pregnant woman who had just discovered the perfect way to lie on her belly.

Stretch Marks

"Look right here," April said, "Do you see anything?"

She had her shirt pulled up just over her belly button, so I could see her round pregnant belly, which by the way, is one of the most beautiful things I've ever seen in my life.

"Right here," she said, pressing her finger against her skin like she was pointing at Spain on a globe.

"Oh, you mean those stretch marks," I said.

"Stretch marks?" April asked, both horrified and curious.

"You have two of them right here," I said, tracing the short blue rivers on her stomach with my finger.

"How long have I had stretch marks?" April asked.

I thought for a second. "I don't know. Maybe two weeks."

April's jaw dropped in complete disbelief. She looked like Munch's *The Scream*.

"Why didn't you tell me?" April asked accusingly. She was craning her neck like an ostrich and trying to see around the other side of her belly. It wasn't working very well.

I smiled. "I guess I thought you knew."

27 WEEKS
Midwife

I'm not sure where I got my assumptions from, but I thought someone only hired a midwife for one of three reasons:

1. You've decided to have the baby at home, in which case a midwife will deliver the baby.
2. You're wealthy enough that you want to hire an extra person to help coordinate your pregnancy—sort of like hiring a wedding planner.
3. You're uptight enough that you want to hire an extra person to keep an eye on your doc while you're in labor to make sure he or she is sticking to your birth plan.

When one of April's friends at the university mentioned she had had a midwife when she gave birth this past fall, we considered getting one for ourselves.

- Not because we've decided to have the baby at home.
- Not because we're wealthy enough to have a personal pregnancy planner.

- Not because we're worried our doctor is going to mess everything up.
- But because we live outside of our home country.

Between learning medical vocabulary in Spanish to working with an unfamiliar health care system to juggling the advice we get from here and abroad, we thought we could use a baby tutor.

Also, we went to our doctor two weeks ago with a list of questions all written out. Our doctor listened intently as we read through the list, and then told us we should ask our midwife those questions.

"Midwife?" we thought, looking at each other.

We arranged to have lunch with Lledón, the midwife April knew about from her friend at school. As we walked with Lledón to the Chinese restaurant just off the university campus, we asked questions. She was incredibly patient with us the entire way. She didn't even hesitate when we asked her to explain the entire birthing process in Spain in detail.

"Are you asking what happens when you have a baby?" she asked.

April smiled.

"No, I'm asking what happens when you have a baby in Spain?" April replied.

It turns out everyone in Spain has a midwife, whether or not we're rich or paranoid. The midwife and the doctor work together as a team to help us have the baby. The midwife is the one who will teach our childbirth class. She's the one who will help us prepare for having the baby and answer all our questions.

In less than an hour we had been enlightened. I felt so much smarter than I had before. Plus, now I liked the idea of having a midwife—I mean if everyone had one anyway. I liked the fact that she would teach our class, answer our questions, and be with us at the hospital.

For some reason, doctors seem busy. Midwives seem available.

Yesterday Lledón called. She's found one of her midwife friends who works with our insurance company and who actually helped Lledón deliver one of her own babies.

Last week I didn't even know we needed a midwife. This week I'll be very happy to meet her.

28 WEEKS, 2 DAYS
Childbirth Class

Our first childbirth class began with a cheerful hello from our midwife and some encouragement to find a spot on one of the comfy blue mats lying on the floor, take off our shoes, and find a relaxing position.

We began our exercises by scrunching up our toes, relaxing them, scrunching them up again, then rotating our ankles in circles.

The whole experience immediately reminded me of a class I took in college called "Voice and Body Warm-ups." I was the only guy who took the class then, and looking around the room at the four pregnant women on mats, I was the only guy taking this class now.

To put things into perspective, at the end of that college class I was absolutely ecstatic to have achieved my personal goal: I had managed to touch my toes without my legs quivering like a newborn calf. The rest of the class, the girls, however, had long moved on to complex yoga positions with such intimidating names as the Salute to the Sun and the Warrior I pose and others I've thankfully managed to forget.

I think it's safe to say most women are more flexible than men, but even most men are like Gumby compared to me. I bend more like an action figure.

I remember going to the physical trainer with a knot in my hamstring after a high school soccer game. After using all but the baseball bat sitting in the corner of the room to work out the knot, she shook her head and wiped her forehead. "You're one of the most inflexible people I've ever worked with," she said.

Anyway, despite the fact that the mats and the gym clothes and the mirrors on the walls all reminded me of my Voice and Body Warm-up days, I nonetheless felt optimistic for one very obvious reason: these women had watermelon bellies. I had the upper hand.

We were lying on our backs doing breathing exercises when our midwife asked us to stand up. I watched these round women struggle to their feet with the same compassion as one watches puppies trying to climb stairs.

"Only a few months," I thought, oozing with empathy, "and you'll be back in the shape you were before."

My only hesitation at this point was that I might get bored. Pregnant women have to do easy exercises, and here I was, a healthy, young guy.

That's about the time things began to change, as I remember it.

We were down on all fours, positioned like a cat, breathing deeply and arching our backs, and I noticed something I hadn't expected. Sweat. I was beading up like a newly waxed car.

Given my history, of course I was concerned. "Oh no," I thought, shammying myself off with my shirt, "I'm getting hot. I'm working too hard."

Our midwife told us to relax, close our eyes, and think of a happy place. The pleasant image of April and myself relaxing over a picnic in a shaded forest without distraction, without bugs, without an uncomfortable bum, which is what I usually remember from picnics, was suddenly interrupted with a comic sketch of me as a human boiler, a heat machine with eyes and ears and a mouth like Mr. Potato Head, and about to explode, shaking violently and billowing with steam that filled the small aerobics room.

"Just don't make me touch my toes," I thought, pleading with our midwife in my head. "I know my body can't handle it, but I'm talking about my ego. We ended on such a good note in college. My ego is like a soft little cuddly bunny that wouldn't hurt anybody—like the Easter bunny. We don't want to hurt the Easter bunny, do we?"

There's only one exercise for me that's worse than touching my toes. It's called the butterfly. Nice name for such a cruel invention. The goal is simple. You sit on your butt, put your feet together so their bottoms are flat against each other, and pull your feet as close to your groin as you can, so in effect, your knees stick out from your body like butterfly wings. Poetic, isn't it?

Next, using your hands or the inside of your elbows, you push your knees as far as you can downward to the mat underneath you, stretching your groin.

The whole experience for me is like prying open a clamshell. You literally have to break the joint holding the two shells together in order to open a clam. The difference is clams are dead. I was not. Not to mention, we are talking about stretching a particularly sensitive part of the male anatomy.

I didn't look like a butterfly. I looked like a junior-high boy, balled up for a cannonball about to hit the water.

I couldn't help but gape at the other women, their bellies light as balloons, fluttering their legs like happy butterflies. I imagined them all laughing and flapping their legs, slowly lifting themselves off their mats and flying away into the cool Mediterranean sky.

The instructor walked slowly around the room observing each of the women. Much to my appreciation, she walked past me without as much as a casual glance, which I can only guess was because of one of two reasons. Either she thought about the fact that I'm a guy and won't be giving birth, so I don't really count anyway, or more likely she realized I was a lost cause and couldn't be bothered with my piddly efforts. Either way, she continued on to where April was sitting and stopped.

April looked bored. She had her knees pinned to the mat with her hands, and occasionally she would flap her knees and do the stretch all over again just for fun.

"In some cases," the instructor said, "some people are too flexible for this particular stretch. You're one of those people. Let me show you the stretch I use. I think it will be more effective for you."

Things got entirely out of hand by the end of the workout. Yes, I was sweating. Yes, I was feeling a burning sensation in many muscles I didn't want to know I had. Yes, my pride was worth as much as a handful of Zimbabwean dollars. But up until this point I had avoided pain.

For our last exercise, our instructor asked us to shake out our arms and shoulders, loosen them up a bit, then one at a time rotate our arms like windmills.

I started with my right arm, and everything went well. The room filled with a flurry of body parts. We switched to our left arm, and everyone began again. I was really getting into this stretch. I could feel my shoulder stretching. As my arm spun faster and faster like a ceiling fan, I focused on relaxing the muscles in my arm, then my rib cage, and finally the shoulder itself. The muscles expanded even more. I felt in complete control of my body.

That's when the clicking began. It sounded like chopsticks breaking or like the pulse of an electric fence if you've ever put your ear close and listened. It sounded painful, and it was. The clicking sound was coming from my shoulder. I didn't know whether to stop flailing my arm or not, so I kept doing it, hoping the problem would work itself out.

It only got worse. Now the clicking sounded like a hammer

on a nail, and people started looking around the room trying to find out where the clicking sound was coming from.

Of course I stopped. I gave up. I rubbed my shoulder. I looked at these women, cheerfully carrying around their sand bags, fluttering their knees like butterflies, whirling their arms like propellers, happy to be in training for the race ahead. And that's when I knew—as if I didn't know before—that there was good reason April was pregnant, and I was not.

29 WEEKS, 2 DAYS
What's a Onesie?

"It's like an undershirt for babies," April said as she folded up a little pink shirt with frills around the sleeves and "little princess" written in blue cursive on the front.

"Okay," I said. I looked at the little white gown I was holding in my hand and placed it on the onesie pile.

"What's a sleeper?" I asked.

April glared at me. "It's what babies sleep in," she said.

I rummaged through the bag of clothes sitting on the floor in front of me until I found something that looked comfortable to sleep in. It had booties, which seemed right, and written again in cursive under a pink butterfly it said, "daddy's little girl." I liked this one.

"And which size goes where again?" I asked, looking at the piles of clothes sitting on the coffee table. They all looked the same. They all looked small.

Kelly, a friend visiting from Madrid, pointed at the piles and said, "0-3 months go here, and 3-6 months go there."

I checked the tag. "3 months," it said.

"What if it says 3 months?" I asked. "3 months could go on either the 0-3 month pile or the 3-6 month pile."

Kelly held out her hand, and I passed her the jacket. She held it up to get a look at it and said, "Definitely 0-3 months." She put the jacket on the pile.

"This one says size 56!" I said. It was the smallest green tank top I had ever seen.

Kelly smiled and reached across the coffee table. I handed it to her.

30 WEEKS, 3 DAYS
Why People Have Kids

If someone had asked me why we decided to start having kids, I would have said, "It just seemed like the right thing to do." Yeah, I realize how nonchalant that sounds, but sometimes the feeling that something is right is all a person needs.

Over the last few months, I've seen this feeling, like a planted seed, grow into something rooted, something leafy, something nourishing. Already, I can't imagine my life without our baby girl. She's developed into a person of her own, already capable of kicking her dad's hand when he's chasing her around mom's belly. Today when I asked myself why we decided to start having kids, I realized that although we had started with a feeling, now our feelings had sprouted into a much clearer image of the family we hoped to be.

The easiest way for me to describe this image was to think of a few reasons people might have kids and cross off the ones that didn't fit. For some reason, defining who I am not is always easier than defining who I am.

We are not having kids because…

The world is a great place to be born, free of crime, poverty and war. I feel much worse about the world these days reading on the BBC about what's happening in Israel and

Palestine. I hate that I don't know what to do about this conflict except watch and pray that it will end soon.

We're financially stable and feel like we can give our kids everything they need. Supposedly, I make enough money to support both of us, our student loans, and the pregnancy on an entry-level web design job. In reality, we eat a lot of rice and beans at the end of the month.

Everyone else is having babies. This may be true for our friends in the small towns in Iowa where April and I grew up, but at age 26, our friends in the city are happy to be single. They're still being kids, not having them.

I'd like to give my kids the life I never had. Fact is, I've had a great life. No complaints. I have no idea what a "great life" will mean for my kids. I think they'll have to figure that out for themselves.

I need an heir to take over the family business. I still don't know what I'm going to be when I grow up. Any ideas?

So, if I take money, power and happiness out of the equation, what am I left with?

What comes to mind are the words of a wise friend of mine. He's my parents' age. We haven't talked in years, but he was someone I could talk to when I was in high school. Occasionally we would grab a coffee from the coffee shop in town and go for a drive, and he would listen to me go on about God and girls and leaving for college.

This friend always had the most predictable answer for everything in life. He would take a sip of his coffee, ponder my questions, and say, "Life is about relationships." That's the only thing I really remember from all our conversations, but it's why I think he's wise because today when I asked myself why I wanted kids, my answer was, "Because life is about relationships."

The kind of relationship a parent has with a child doesn't

come around very often. They're the exception. They're the limited edition. They're like a good bottle of wine, a gaze at the Grand Canyon, or a first kiss.

Granted, once April and I have kids, we won't be able to get rid of them. We take that chance. But in exchange we'll get the whole works. In the end, we'll spend more time with our parents and children and grandchildren than anyone else on the planet. We'll talk more openly and more directly with our kids, even if it takes us years, because if we don't, we'll rot like bad fruit. And whether we love our kids or hate them or ignore them, we will still be central characters in their story.

To be family is to be in the most intense kind of relationship there is. To be family is to be a witness to someone's life and to bring meaning to it.

30 WEEKS, 5 DAYS

It Takes A Village to Raise a Child

I really thought the reason we came to Madrid this weekend was so April could do research for her thesis. However, as we sat on a park bench at the playground in Plaza Olavide watching dads push their kids on swings and little boys tumble down the slide together and land in a pile at the bottom, I wondered if we had come here for another kind of research.

I had tagged along with April this morning for a visit to an intercultural mediation group. Afterwards, we had some time to kill, so we got a map from the tourist office and sat down on a bench. We found ourselves looking at the map of the city with our baby eyes, pointing out the neighborhoods and squares where we remembered seeing families with kids while we were living in Madrid.

We followed our map down the streets of Madrid like a baby compass until we wandered into Plaza Olavide and got held up by a traffic jam of baby buggies. The sound of children playing on the playground was as welcoming as chirping seagulls at the beach, and at the same time, I was overwhelmed with loneliness. April's classes had ended eight weeks ago, and most of our Masters friends had scattered as suddenly as if a bag of pasta had been knocked on the floor.

All the pregnancy books say it's best to fight the urge to make any major life changes during pregnancy, so even though we no longer had any reason to stay living in Castellón, we had decided to stay put for our own sanity until the baby was born. Still, I was haunted by the abyss of uncertainty at the end of this adventure. The future was a black hole, a bottomless pit.

In contrast, Madrid was concrete and tangible. My heart ached to see all these families living here. Obviously they had decided that they belonged in this spot, and that they had claimed this playground as their own. I wanted a place to imagine my family.

April and I talked at the playground, and later at our friends' apartment, with the same intensity as when we had started dating. I felt like we were getting to know ourselves again for the first time, now as parents.

We had originally talked about moving anywhere where April could begin her career in mediation after she finished her studies. Now, starting a career with a newborn sounded overly ambitious. Moving to a place where we had never lived sounded isolating. We were starting a family, and it didn't make sense to try to start a career or find a new community at the same time, especially when we already had jobs and a supportive community waiting for us in Madrid.

April and I had moved around a lot. We hadn't lived in the same spot for more than two years. Each move provided a chance to start over again and see the world from a different angle. Now that our little one was on the way, however, I was beginning to understand what people meant when they said they were settling down. It meant they recognized that they wouldn't have as much time for themselves when they had kids, and instead of having time to move to interesting places and find new jobs and build new friendships, they were going to have to rely on what they already had, so that they could focus most of their time on their family.

I was beginning to think of Madrid as solid ground we could build on.

So, we've decided to move back to Madrid. After the baby is born, the plan is to spend four months in Iowa with our families before I start back at my old job in Madrid as one of the pastors at an international church. My office will be at home, and April will be a stay-at-home mom, at least for a little while.

I guess technically we've followed the advice of the pregnancy books and resisted the urge to make any major life changes during pregnancy, but as soon as the baby is born, our life is going to look a lot like a mobile dangling over a crib—lots of moving parts. Hopefully the end result is we will be in a place where we already have jobs and friends and plenty of time to get to know our little girl.

31 WEEKS

Monkeys as Blue as Superman Ice Cream

Our friends Robyn and Samuel and their one-and-half-year-old Josiah are staying with us for two weeks.

They've lived in Spain for a couple of years and recently relocated to Seville. If there's one thing you should know about Seville it's that it's the last place on earth you would want to be in August because of the heat. It's like a prison. The only way to survive is to lock yourself in your room, pull the shades, and sit in front of the fan.

So, when August rolls around, people in Seville scatter like pigeons. They get buddy-buddy with their friends who live on the coast.

Lucky for us, we happen to be those friends. Samuel and Robyn will be staying with us, and then moving on to our other friends Jesús and Rachel, who also live on the Spanish coast.

Yesterday I went to the library to get movies and Robyn came along. We walked in the front door and Robyn said, "I'll be in here," pointing at the "Kids Books" sign.

I went upstairs, spent about as much time to find a movie as it would take to watch *7 Years in Tibet* because I'm incredibly indecisive about these sorts of things, and finally returned to the ground floor to find Robyn. I half expected her to be asleep at one of the reading tables or to have simply given up on me and walked home.

Instead, I found her standing next to one of the reading tables with a pile of books equal to the stack on April's desk for her Masters thesis. Robyn was flipping through a picture book, completely engaged.

I almost didn't want to interrupt. She looked fascinated. But she saw me at the door, so I walked over.

"Did you find anything?" I asked, looking once again at the stack of children's books.

"I found all kinds of books," she said, "even Samuel's favorite." I noticed she mentioned Samuel, her husband, not Josiah, her toddler.

She picked up the book, the title was *Where's My Mother?*, and began paging through the glossy pages of green crocodiles with red button eyes, monkeys as blue as superman ice cream, and pudgy elephants, tiptoeing in front of a violet sky.

We checked out the books with my card, and I handed them to Robyn as we left the building. Something about the exchange of books from my hands to hers felt unsettling, like one of us had just gotten off the teeter-totter.

Here I was holding two DVDs that were, at best, "just okay," and Robyn was holding children's books. That's when it slapped me in the face. Robyn was holding the very essence of childhood—innocence, curiosity, simplicity, playfulness—in her hands, in tangible form, like some kind of Rosetta Stone.

Robyn read from *Where's My Mother?* as we walked home, reciting its poetry from memory. It was obvious that she had studied these words until they had made sense to her again, until she was a fluent speaker in the mysterious languages of childhood that I had lost when the dust of adulthood had settled.

I wanted the book too, like one toddler grabbing a toy from another. I wanted to hold this key to childhood in my hand, to see it and use it, to unlock the most childish and foolish parts of me.

Like most, I suppose, I've spent a lot of time trying to be a grown up, trying to be professional and put together. But wasn't there always plenty of time for that? As I listened to Robyn read, I felt like I had been missing out on being childish again. I wanted to play too.

Children's books make us like children again, but how much more do our own children who beg us to jump on the bed and blow bubbles and stick out our tongues? They give us an excuse to be all these beautiful things that children are.

31 WEEKS, 2 DAYS
Fireflies

"Do you ever get sick of talking about being pregnant?" Kim asked.

Kim and April sat chatting at the kitchen table while I pushed chapati dough around in a skillet and watched it make bubbles.

"No," April said, "I don't talk about it that much."

April and I don't actually talk about being pregnant that much, at least not as much as I expected. Sometimes, especially in the first few months, we talked about being pregnant so little I forgot about it completely.

A few months ago I was talking to my dad about what we could do while my parents were visiting, and I said, "Well, we could go to the amusement park. April and I love roller coasters."

My dad hesitated, thinking out loud. "I don't think you can ride roller coasters when you're pregnant."

"Oh, right," I said. I didn't add, "Funny, I actually forgot April was pregnant there for a minute. Oops!"

I think God gave pregnant women big bellies for people like me. Pregnant bellies are like giant sticky notes.

Anyway, I would have answered Kim's question differently than April did. In fact, I did. I said I wasn't sick of talking about the pregnancy because our conversations were constantly changing as we tried to keep up with the little baby growing in April's belly. We discussed the pregnancy test, then our first doctor's appointment, then the ultrasound, then finding a midwife, then childbirth class, then picking baby names, and now we were already in the last trimester, and theoretically, we were supposed be prepared to have a baby at any time.

When April and I get a chance to talk about the baby, I feel like it's more of a necessity than a pastime. I feel like I'm cramming for a big exam, and believe me, there are some big baby handbooks out there. I have one sitting right next to me here on the nightstand. It's called *The Baby Book*. I think it probably weighs more than most babies at birth.

If I could change my thinking, though, I'd do it. When I was a kid, and my family would visit my grandparents on their farm in Illinois, my brother and sister and I used to run outside at dusk with canning jars and catch fireflies. We would put the jars next to our beds, and after pulling on our pajamas and turning off the lights, we would lie in our beds and watch the fireflies dance.

I'd like to think that each conversation we have about our beautiful little girl and her journey into this world is like catching one more firefly in a jar. We collect these glowing embers, pieces of the mystery and the miracle of birth, and we somehow try to contain them in our words, even if just for one night, to see them up close.

31 WEEKS, 5 DAYS
Heat

I woke up this morning, wandered into the living room, and found April sleeping on the couch with the door to the balcony open and a fan blowing on her face.

I got the hint that April was feeling warmish a few weeks ago when she began taking cold showers during the night. I'd wake up in the dim light of morning to the sound of water running through the pipes.

Then there was the day April cried. She was at her desk collecting thoughts about her thesis in a Word document, and she overheated. Tears sizzled on her cheeks as she sat in silence.

She had been so brave about the whole thing, choosing not to complain, but instead to get creative about how to stay cool. I just knew today she had had enough. With all this heat, she was wondering how she would ever finish writing her thesis by her due date on October 3.

We tried to make things better. Friday afternoon we headed down to the beach with our friend Amy who was visiting from

Madrid. We've gotten in the habit of going to the beach later in the day, after six o'clock, so we can enjoy the coolness of a tempered sun and the welcome breeze from the sea.

We soaked in the water and napped on our towels. I woke up refreshed, but April woke up worse than before. The problem was she was supposed to be cool on the beach. I was cool. Amy was cool. The breeze was undeniably present, hushing the heat, but it wasn't enough. April's skin felt like a warm washcloth.

As we waited for the bus to go home, an older woman reached into her purse and took out a Spanish fan. With the flip of her wrist, she spread the fan, like peacock feathers, and began waving it in her face.

April smiled. Maybe there was hope after all. The thought of buying a fan at the dollar store was enough of a boost that Saturday morning April woke up with determination. She looked feisty.

April had decided that we would not go to our usual weekend breakfast place. Instead, we would go to the Teapot, a pleasant little café in a square only a few blocks away. We arrived, and immediately I knew what April had in mind. This café had cold air for sale.

We walked past tables of people inside the café reading their morning newspaper and sat for hours under the air conditioner. April contentedly sipped her drink and said we would have to come again.

Today is Monday. April and I look forward to Mondays because for two hours in the evening we get to go to our childbirth class in an air conditioned building. We count on it.

Walking into that building is like flipping a switch. We turn off temperature. We take it out of the equation. We chat. We exercise. We discuss baby things. The thought never crosses our mind that we are hot or cold. To think that somewhere someone is letting something as unobtrusive as air get in the way of having a good day seems silly.

So this afternoon we walked to class with as much purpose as explorers headed for the North Pole. We arrived to find our midwife standing outside the front door of the building. She was leaning against her car. She looked hot.

She was talking to one of the women in our class and telling her that we would not be having class this evening because she had some family business to take care of. She said goodbye, got in her car, and drove off.

The two of us were left standing there in the street, and suddenly I felt very warm. In fact, I felt hotter than I had felt all summer. Standing in that small street between buildings, I felt like a piece of bread wedged in a toaster. I was sweating like cheese.

At that moment I understood how April had been feeling all week: too hot to do anything, and too hot to do anything about it.

"Well, I know one thing," April said, matter-of-factly, "we'll have to go find air conditioning somewhere else tonight."

I was melting like ice cream, but April was considering our options. She had been hot all week, and now was no exception. She had put up with being a few degrees hotter than everyone else in the room. She had put up with a meltdown and being too hot to do anything about it. She had put up with finding any way she could to stay cool. As a result, she was handling it. She seemed okay.

April took my hand in hers, and we began walking down the street.

"Come on," she said, "let's go to the Teapot and drink tea under the air conditioner."

Camino de Santiago

"If I told you giving birth wasn't painful, I would be lying to you."

I should have thought something was up when our midwife said this. I think she was trying to give a disclaimer for the VHS tape she was putting in the VCR.

The film appeared in black in white on a small television sitting on a shelf in a cupboard at one end of our classroom. April and I sat with two other women on folding chairs.

The only reason I could think of that they would show us such an outdated film was because in the old days they would show things they wouldn't show anymore.

The film began with a pleasant image of a pregnant English woman walking through a pasture in the evening wearing a wool sweater and softly rubbing circles on her belly.

In a matter of minutes, however, the English woman was strapped to a hospital bed, bracing herself, and howling at the moon. She made Neve Campbell in *Scream* sound like a kitten. From the next room, you wouldn't have known if we were watching a birthing video or *The Texas Chainsaw Massacre*.

The close-up of the baby's head emerging from inside his mother did not help matters. I caught myself about to say out-loud, "Go back inside! This isn't working!"

But, of course, over time with lots of pushing and panting and pleading the baby was squeezed into this world. The camel had passed through the eye of the needle.

I had the thought I imagine every new father has but doesn't say, "How did that come from there?"

Pain. That's how.

I'm not sure if this will sound far-fetched, but the only way I feel okay about sending my wife into the painful experience of childbirth and not scheduling a c-section tomorrow is thinking about April and I walking the Camino de Santiago together last summer.

The Camino de Santiago is a pilgrimage to Santiago de Compostela in the northern province of Galicia in Spain. People have walked to this town from all over the world for centuries, and last summer April and I walked around twelve miles a day for eleven days through rain and sunshine, from morning until evening, and through forests, mountains and villages to reach our final destination.

Walking to Santiago is one of my most cherished experiences, but only because it was also one of the most difficult April and I have ever done together. Within two days, April was limping because of a bad knee, and I was hobbling on a sore arch. We spent hours each morning sticking band-aids, wrapping ankles, running needle and thread through blisters and massaging cramped muscles. We experienced pain from the beginning of the trip to the end. It never let up. We often thought about giving up and taking the bus home, and at least once every day we said we would never do this again.

Somehow, though, God uses difficult situations to bring people together. He's like a beggar rummaging through the trash until he finds something he can use. I am thankful for the opportunity I had to see April persevere through such a physically demanding adventure. We helped each other along the way, sometimes arm in arm, sometimes just walking side by side in silence, but somehow growing closer together and learning so much about each other, including the simple fact that we could do it. We could walk all that way.

I trust April will handle the pain of childbirth okay because I've seen her handle pain before. I know she can do it. And I imagine going through the difficulty of childbirth with our baby girl will only bring us all closer together.

Wedding Ring

"Do you wear a wedding ring?" my friend Rogier asked me on Friday. Rogier is the father of three.

I showed him the white gold band around my finger.

"I only have one piece of advice for you when your wife goes into labor," Rogier said. "Don't wear your wedding ring."

"Why not?" I asked.

Rogier held up his hand with the shiny gold band around one finger. He took his other hand and squeezed it around his left hand, his ring disappearing behind his knuckles.

"It hurts," Rogier said, "when your wife is having contractions, and she grabs your hand." He smiled and raised his eyebrows as if to say, "You'll see."

"Trust me. When your wife is in that much pain, the last thing you're going to say to her is 'Honey, you're squeezing my hand, and it hurts.'"

Benchwarmers

Justin sat back in his chair and sighed. "I don't sleep well anymore," he said.

I laughed. "Me neither."

"It's like my body knows the baby is coming," Justin said.

You would have thought we were two pregnant women commiserating, but in fact, our pregnant wives were sitting at the table next to us.

We met up with our friends Justin and Jen at a conference we're attending. They're our age and also having their first.

Naturally, when the rest of our friends at the conference got sick of us blabbing on an on about being pregnant and found better things to do with their time, we found ourselves—the four parent wannabes—walking over to the dining hall together and talking shop.

April and Jen launched into a conversation about how hot it is everywhere, and to be fair, Europe is toasty this summer, while Justin and I sat down at a table with our trays of food, not quite sure where to begin.

Being the husband, I imagine, is a lot like being a benchwarmer for Real Madrid. Of course you're an important person if you play for one of the most decorated soccer teams in the world. Not only are you kicking the ball around with the likes of Casillas and Raúl and Sergio Ramos, the list goes on, but you work hard with them in practice and, in a way, you keep them in shape for the big games.

But, you're a benchwarmer. When it comes down to it, you're not the one running out onto the field.

Especially now that we're in the last minutes of the game, or the last trimester of the pregnancy, I can see how different April's experience is from mine. Every day she plays more of the game, lugging her belly around, dodging mood swings, anticipating snack times, and pacing herself. She is the star, and she deserves every bit of credit for how hard she plays.

Still, it was nice to see Justin, a benchwarmer just like me.

We talked about our experiences of the pregnancy, and I began to see that somewhere along the line the pregnancy had changed us too. We were becoming dads. We had just been too busy watching the game to notice.

34 WEEKS, 6 DAYS

Castor Oil

"Castor oil and a long walk worked every time," Kari said. "I was in labor by the end of the day."

Kari is a friend of ours, and an expert at having babies—she had five. Not only did she have five babies, but she also had five boys, all of which had her waddling by four months. Her first baby was nine and a half pounds, and they only got bigger from there. By her third she had discovered a sure-fire way to self-induce labor. Drink a bottle of castor oil and go for a long walk. Two weeks before her due date, she would self-induce, just before her boys would bulk up.

April was only five months pregnant when Kari gave us her family recipe for self-inducing labor, and I remember not paying much attention to it at the time. It seemed almost irrelevant then, in the same way my older sister used to tell me when I was in grade school that someday I would like girls. Like that would ever happen!

Today, however, is a different story. I'm sitting here on our balcony enjoying the evening breeze off the Mediterranean, and I'm thinking about castor oil.

The problem is I want my daughter to be here now. I don't want to wait. And it's so much worse that she's right there in April's belly. I'm the little kid eyeing his present under the tree, who can't wait for Christmas morning. The only difference is I'm an adult, and I'm capable of devising all kinds of elaborate plots to get our baby out faster.

I keep trying to remind myself that babies know when

they're supposed to come. As a rule, hurrying things up is a bad idea. And, as much as I hate to say it, waiting is good for me. John Ortberg says, "Waiting is not just something we have to do until we get what we want. Waiting is part of the process of becoming what God wants us to be."

I can't help it though. April and I already take long walks together every day. The only thing I'd have to do is slip some castor oil into her orange juice in the morning.

35 WEEKS, 2 DAYS
Hospital

We visited the hospital yesterday. Well, first we had to find it. Our doctor had told us we would be having the baby at the private hospital since we had private health insurance. What she didn't tell us was where the private hospital was, and we never thought to ask. I guess it never occurred to us that we didn't even know where the hospital was until we decided to go there.

Thankfully only two hospitals were listed in the phone book, and one of them was called "The General Hospital." We decided to go to the other one.

Maybe you're wondering how we got this far along in the pregnancy without knowing where the hospital was. You might say we were being irresponsible.

Of course we were. We were purposely avoiding the hospital. We had discovered recently that too much information could be a bad thing, and as a result, we had adopted a new family policy: What you don't know can't hurt you.

It all started a few weeks back at the dinner table when I made the mistake of asking April, "What's your worst fear about giving birth?" and then she told me, and we both felt like we had been dragged into an alley and beaten up.

I wished at that moment that April hadn't read all those

pregnancy books. Now she had more opinions than she knew what to do with, and instead of being helpful, these opinions had brought into focus an image of the ideal birth that could never be. April had eaten from the Tree of Knowledge of Good and Evil.

April's worst fear was that she would be "stuck" on the operating table and not be allowed to move around or try different positions to help give birth, which her books told her would either lead to extreme unnecessary pain or worse, a c-section.

April began talking about her worst fear constantly, and I felt increasingly more responsible and helpless. Deep down, I knew there was very little I could do to change the situation. Ultimately, the doctor would make the decision, and here in Spain, that meant giving birth on an operating table.

We were destined to fail.

We arrived at the hospital with a long list of questions, but I was aware that we really only needed the one question answered. We had decided to visit the hospital in the end because our fear had cornered us, and we had no choice but to look it in the eye. Our due date was coming, and we needed to know which hospital to go to and what would happen when we got there.

At the front desk I told the secretary we would be having our baby at this hospital and asked if we could have a look around.

"You mean a tour?" she asked. "We're not a travel agency."

"Um...okay" I said. "So I guess taking a tour of this hospital is not something people normally do?"

"No," she said, "that is not something people normally do."

I thought for a second.

"Well, we're not from here," I said. "We're not familiar with how hospitals work here. Do you think you can ask someone if we can take a tour, or even if we can just see one of the hospital rooms where new mothers would stay?"

She bit her lip trying not to smirk. "I'll see what I can do."

She picked up the phone. "Yeah. I have some people here who want to see a room." She listened, then looked at me. "Alright. I'll send them up."

She put down the phone.

"Second floor."

We stepped off the elevator and walked to the nurse's station. One of the nurses met us at the counter with a smile and asked, "Are you the ones who would like to see the maternity suite?"

"Yes," we said.

"Alright. Follow me."

She unlocked a door at the end of the hall, and we followed her into the suite. There was a small living room and a door that led into a bedroom. The couch along the wall converted into a bed. There was plenty of room.

"Anything else?" the nurse asked after we had taken a few moments to look around.

I frowned. Whatever it was we were looking for, it wasn't here.

"Can we see the delivery room?" I asked.

"No, I'm sorry," the nurse apologized. "We can't allow that."

As soon as she said the words, I realized the reason we had come to the hospital was to see the delivery room. That was the room April was afraid of, and that's where we would find our fears growing like mold in a forgotten Tupperware. Our fears were sealed in the delivery room two floors beneath us, and we had no way of doing battle with them. We were stuck.

We did have the nurse, however, and she had been in the delivery room before. And we still had our question, and she probably had an answer.

"I do have one question," I said as I pulled a small notebook from my back pocket and flipped through the pages.

The nurse smiled.

"Do women normally give birth on an operating table at this hospital?"

"Yes."

"So they have to stay in their beds the whole time?"

"Yes"

"And they're not allowed to change positions or get up and move around?"

"That's right."

I stopped and looked at April. I had no more questions. I wished I had more—some way of asking our way out of the inevitable truth that April's worst fear had become a reality and that there was nothing I could do about it.

"Any more questions?" the nurse asked as she walked over to the door.

April bit her lip and shook her head fiercely as the tears cut jagged lines across her cheeks.

36 WEEKS

Handbook to Bad Parenting

I'm all about bad parenting books because most of the time after reading something utopian like *The Baby Book*, I feel like the best April and I could do is the moment the baby is born, bundle her up in swaddling clothes and hand her off to the nuns at the convent down the street. Let *them* do God's work on the child.

Anne Lamott is a favorite. Of course her son Sam is in college now, but when he was born, she wrote *Operating Instructions*, which is exactly what I was looking for—an unedited, unpolished, un-the-way-things-*should*-be kind of baby book—and I love it. Why? Because there's something comforting, something so warm and snuggly like being wrapped in a receiving blanket about knowing that someone else is more messed up than I am—even if I'm close.

Just for fun, here are a few lines from Lamott's book:

> I'm so tired that I could easily go to sleep at 8:30 and sleep for twelve hours, but instead I walk the sobbing baby and think my evil thoughts—Lady Macbeth as a nanny.

> The worst night yet…If I had a baseball bat, I would smash holes in the wall.

> Real tears leave his eyes now. It is almost more than I can take. Before, he'd be sobbing but there were no tears. Now there are. It seems an unfair advantage.

> I'm not even remotely well enough to be a mother. That's what the problem is. Also, I don't think I like babies.

Another favorite is dooce.com by Heather Armstrong. Even before April and I were thinking about having kids, when I really had nothing in common with a stay-at-home mother from Utah, I was reading Heather's blog and marveling over how very terrifying parenthood really is. Heather says it all, and then she laughs…and then you laugh. It's amazing.

And so, I thought, maybe today I would give you some bad parenting. It's my first shot. Unfortunately, I probably won't swear as eloquently as Anne Lamott or tell you off as well as Heather Armstrong could. But, I can tell you the truth.

The truth is that for me this past week has been the hardest week of the pregnancy so far. Something about going to the hospital last Thursday put everything in motion. Before that point, the pregnancy was theoretical. It looked good on paper. But once April and I were standing there together in the maternity suite, I knew this was for real, and I felt like Atlas carrying the weight of the world on his shoulders.

Part of the burden is I want to be a human shield for my pregnant wife. She goes around the house with her bumper belly looking cute and cuddly like a puppy or a hamster that needs to be held and fed and pampered. Don't get me wrong. She's a big girl. She's handling all of this better than I am. But I feel like I need to protect her from the world, and I just can't do it. By the end of the day, I'm wrung out like a washcloth. All I'm good for is watching TV.

I also feel like having a baby is all about logistics and meeting an ambitious deadline. It's like being the Stage Manager for the next Broadway show. I'm responsible for making sure the lights are working, the props are in place, the actors are happy and know their lines, and that the right people are there to see opening night.

Okay, I'm not sure a Stage Manager does all those things, but the fact is I feel like I have to be an administrative genius to have a baby. And if there's one thing you should know about me, it's that I'm not very good at doing more than one thing at once.

I don't want to be overwhelmed. I want to be strong and in control. I feel weak because April is handling the last few weeks of the pregnancy better than me, which seems backwards.

I wanted to be able to protect April from her fears and anxieties about giving birth, but finally I've had to shimmy the white flag up the pole and admit that I don't actually have much control over the end of the pregnancy. I can't guarantee the birth will go well, and I can't stop April from worrying.

So, this afternoon I did the only thing left I know how to do. I went to the beach looking for Jesus. I left April reading a book on her towel and went for a walk along the water. The waves washed away my cluttered thoughts so I could listen better, and there was Jesus waiting for me, like he always does, which is why I trust him.

I stopped to watch a little girl, doggie paddling out to sea. She looked helpless against the waves that lifted her up and down. At times she disappeared completely out of sight. Still, she didn't look worried, but determined. She was confident that her dad, who reclined nearby on his towel reading a novel, would be at her side in an instant if she cried, "Daddy!"

I guess I just needed to know that the further that April and I got from shore, Jesus was still there watching us, capable of being at our side in an instant. I laughed to myself as I imagined Jesus as David Hasselhoff in *Baywatch* running shirtless in red swimming trunks down the beach to our rescue.

36 WEEKS, 6 DAYS

Hurricanes and Puppy Love

I had two dreams last night.

Dream One: The Hurricane
In my first dream April and I were hiking with a group of

people to the top of a volcano on a deserted island. April was eight months pregnant, like she is in real life, and seemed to be keeping up with the rest of the group, even though the island itself was like a pile of rocks tangled in jungle brush.

Near the top of the volcano the wind changed directions. I couldn't make out what the people hiking in front of me were saying, but I could tell they were worried about something.

In a matter of minutes the wind was blowing so strongly we could barely keep our footing. The sky began churning overhead and the water turned black. We were in a hurricane.

Everyone in the group began climbing faster and looking for shelter from the storm. We scattered off in different directions, each thinking only of self-preservation.

The ground underneath my feet began to shake, and suddenly I was seized with fear. I had left April behind. Just as I looked over my shoulder and saw her bracing herself between two rocks, the ground between us crumbled, literally splitting the island into two halves.

April began to cry as both halves of the island began slowly drifting apart, the canyon between us growing impossibly wide.

Dream Two: Puppy Love

April and I were in Madrid visiting our friend Mathilda whose dog was giving birth. Her dog's name is Kim, and she's a poodle.

Kim was giving birth in a hospital like most women do in Spain. She had an IV in her arm. Her contractions were being monitored.

Nothing about this seems unusual, except that she looked ridiculously small to be in that hospital bed.

Mathilda stood next to Kim, telling her to push, wiping the sweat off her forehead, and tightly holding Kim's small little paw in her fist.

The doctor was about to deliver the baby when he said, "I

need someone to catch the baby." He looked around the room. "Now!" he said. Everyone looked at me, so I stepped forward.

Kim pushed once more, whimpered, and the baby slid into my hands. "It's a girl," the doctor said and cut the umbilical cord.

I cradled the puppy in my arms and noticed how blood-shot her eyes were. It didn't matter. She was the cutest puppy in the world.

Observations:

1. Laurie is staying with us for a week before she heads to Philadelphia to begin her next job as a history teacher. Last night before we went to bed she called her parents in Florida to see if they had evacuated for Hurricane Ernesto.
2. Yesterday, out of the blue, April asked me, "Are you afraid of me going into labor?"
3. April says I may be feeling guilty for thinking puppies are cuter than babies, which is true by the way. I do think puppies are cuter than babies, hands down.

Care to interpret?

37 WEEKS, 1 DAY

Margo

I made the mistake of telling our friend Margo a few days ago that we still hadn't figured out how we were going to get to the hospital when April went into labor. Not to say that Margo didn't have a right to be concerned, to be visibly but politely fascinated by our lack of preparation less than three weeks before our due date. April and I talked as if it was the first time we had even thought about how we were going to get to the hospital.

We don't own a car, I pointed out, so maybe we should call

for a taxi. But then again, the taxi service has never been very reliable in Castellón, especially not early in the morning.

"Maybe we'll walk," April suggested.

Margo's eyes went round.

Ever since that day, the day April mentioned waddling to the hospital, Margo's been telling us how laid back we are about everything. She says she could never be like us because we don't worry about things.

I don't think it helped any when we invited Margo over for chocolate chip cookies last week and casually mentioned that our baby is going to sleep in a trunk.

"A what?" Margo asked, nearly choking on her cookie.

"A trunk," I said. "You know. A container for holding things—in this case, a baby."

"Here, I'll show you," April said. She and Margo walked to our bedroom at the other end of the apartment and looked at the trunk.

"Well, at least it doesn't have a lid," Margo pointed out, trying to be optimistic.

"Yeah, Kelly took it off with a screwdriver," April replied.

Margo smiled apologetically.

"What?" April asked.

"I thought it was going to look like a little coffin," she confessed.

Maybe Margo had a point. Maybe only laid-back people would put their baby to sleep in a trunk. It seemed sturdy to me.

But the thing is, I don't feel laid back. I feel lots of things, but definitely not serenity, not peace of mind, not like I've been soaking in an Arabic bath or anything.

My list of descriptors sounds more like something you would read in the fine print at the bottom of a drug prescription. I don't sleep well. I'm tired. I can't concentrate. I'm even jumpy. I was stirring rice in the kitchen the other day when April came up behind me, put her arms around my chest, and I sprang like a grasshopper.

I've never experienced an excitement and anticipation as strong as this one. I'm like a dog who hears the key in the lock.

And you know what, Margo helps. Her belief that I'm as calm as the Mediterranean is just what I need right now. I need to be lied to. Sometimes what we need is someone else to tell us that we are the thing we're not. Speaking it might just make it come true.

37 WEEKS, 6 DAYS
Babymoon

I was talking with my friend Jeannette recently. She has a two-year-old daughter. She was telling me that her daughter was born around Christmas time, and she and her husband had plans to spend Christmas Day with her family.

By the time Christmas Day came around, Jeannette wasn't looking forward to the day at all. She was tired from recovering from her pregnancy and taking care of the baby. All she wanted was her family to pamper her a little bit, but she just knew that when they arrived at her parents' house, everyone would want to see the baby, and no one would even notice her.

Sure enough, they arrived at Jeannette's parents' house, Grandma took the baby, and everyone crowded around. No one asked Jeannette how she was doing much less said hello to her.

Within a few minutes she left the room and cried out her frustration in the hallway.

Of course Jeannette was telling me her story two years after that Christmas Day, and she was laughing about it, laughing at herself for all the new feelings that come with being a new parent.

Saturday was my 27th birthday. April surprised me on Friday with a two-day trip to Valencia, which is the closest big city to where we live.

We love to travel. Some of our favorite memories together are weekend trips we've taken to different cities in Spain like Salamanca and Cuenca and Alicante. Since we've been pregnant, we haven't taken a weekend trip, so April figured this was our last chance to go for a weekend with just the two of us.

I was listening to a radio show yesterday called *The Parent's Journal,* and the person they were interviewing on the show actually had a name for this kind of trip. He called it a "babymoon" instead of a "honeymoon."

Since we moved near Valencia a year ago, I've been talking to April about going to this nature preserve called the Albufera Nature Park just outside of Valencia. This park is special because many of the birds that migrate between Africa and Northern Europe stop there during their trip.

I'm not a bird watcher. In fact, I would put most birds at this park into three self-named categories: bird, duck and stork. I don't really have any vocabulary beyond that. But, I'm always up for something new, so I thought it would be interesting to go and see the birds, and do as bird people do.

We've had a number of people tell us about this park. All of them have suggested the same itinerary:

1. Arrive at the park around lunchtime.
2. Have a paella, a traditional rice dish, on the beach.
3. Finally, go for a boat ride around the lake, preferably at sunset, and enjoy watching the birds.

We thought we would follow tradition, so we set off before lunch in search of a paella on the beach. To save money, we skipped the Bus Turístic and got on a local bus that was going to the same place, the Albufera Nature Park. The lady at the tourist office said there was really only one bus stop for the park, and we would know it when we saw it. However, as we began passing road signs that said we were already in the park and making a number of stops along the highway, I thought I better ask someone.

I like old people, so I asked the ones sitting in front of us. They were very helpful. The one lady in particular immediately began sketching maps in the air with a scurry of hand gestures, singing her directions with the authority of an opera soloist, and of course having no doubt in her mind that I was understanding everything she was saying, even though she was speaking Valenciano, a mixture of Spanish and French.

All we really needed to know, however, was that when she got off the bus at the next stop and beckoned for us to follow, we should get off the bus too.

With a hand on my shoulder, she led us down a dirt path to a restaurant.

"Eat here," she said, wagging her finger at the restaurant.

"When you're finished, go back to the highway and follow it to the stop light. There you will find the boats."

She smiled at both of us, squeezed my arm once more for good measure, and said, "*Hasta luego*," before walking off in the direction of the apartment building to our left.

April looked at the restaurant, then at the dirt path, and then at me.

"I don't think we're in the right place," she said thoughtfully.

"I don't see the beach." She peered down the dirt path at the highway, busy with traffic.

"I don't see the lake." We both looked past the restaurant at the sparse collection of apartment buildings that stretched my definition of a pueblo.

"And I don't think this restaurant serves paella." The restaurant looked more like a gas station with food. Three girls stood at the doorway licking ice cream.

This was the critical moment in our trip, where if I had had Doc Brown's time-traveling De Lorean in *Back to the Future*, I would have set the dials on the dashboard to this moment. I would have gone back in time and told myself that the forecast for the future was no good and it was in our best interest to get back on the bus and go home.

Instead, we felt adventurous. It almost felt biblical, you know, like we were Mary and Joseph looking for a place to lay our heads. The only small difference was Mary and Joseph did actually know where they were going. They were from Bethlehem.

In contrast, we had the same lack of information as, say, Christopher Columbus, who set sail from Spain and thought he had reached India when he had actually reached the Americas.

We had the same fatalistic determination as Sir John Franklin and his fellow Englishmen who meant to find the Northwest Passage through North America's Arctic Ocean, spurred on by their belief that "it's gotta be just beyond that white part" and were found years later, preserved like flies in ice cubes, in excellent condition for the explorers after them to adequately document their failure.

We were also as fit for the adventure as Bill Bryson's companion Katz was for the Appalachian Trail in *A Walk in the Woods*. I was breaking in new shoes, or more accurately, my new shoes were breaking me in. More importantly, April was eight-and-a-half-months pregnant. She waddles everywhere now, by the way.

All this to say, we were in much worse shape than we realized.

Back at the highway, two women at the bus stop confirmed that the boats were indeed just down the road and to the right, maybe a 10-minute walk.

We set off. We reached the intersection the older woman and the women at the bus stop had talked about, and to our relief, we could see the lake. It was right there on the other side of the highway, although somewhat fenced in by reeds and trees. *The boats must be very close*, we thought to ourselves.

We crossed the intersection and walked to the right, following the highway that ran along the lake. Like mail carriers in route, we walked purposefully down the highway. At least for twenty minutes or so, and then we hesitated. We put our hands on our hips. We felt the sun burning our backs. April looked tired like she had just carried a bag of concrete from the restaurant.

Still, there was that one building we could see just past the trees, maybe another ten minutes down the road. We'd come this far already. We had too much invested to turn around.

I questioned my judgment then, and I question my judgment now as the husband of a very pregnant wife walking down the shoulder of a busy highway. Images I had seen on TV of a highway patrolman standing on the side of the road writing up a ticket and getting hit by a pickup truck in oncoming traffic kept stamping my brain.

Even worse, we arrived at the building, and instead of being a small port with boats, it was a supply shed for the local fire department.

We no longer looked ambitious. We looked tired. We looked like two people who wished we were at home sitting on the couch together watching a movie or reading a book. I wished it wasn't my birthday, and that it was just a normal day.

Like cars out of gas coasting into the station on fumes, we made our way back to the restaurant. The boats were out of the picture for the moment. We were thinking about survival now. We needed something to eat.

I felt like we were eating money at that restaurant. The food was expensive, the kind of expensive where the restaurant has nothing really to offer except that they're the only restaurant around, so you either eat there, or you eat nowhere. I also felt like I was eating money because money isn't food, and this food wasn't really food either. It tasted like paper greased by a thousand hands.

We didn't say much over lunch. We didn't think much either. We just sat there.

It's fair to say we really hadn't walked that long. Maybe an hour. But watching us walk that highway was like watching two ants cross a sidewalk. For any person, crossing a sidewalk is a matter of one or two steps. For those ants, it's like crossing the Sahara.

Eventually, we did find perspective, but not that day. That day I felt a lot like my friend Jeannette on Christmas Day, squeezing out tears in the hallway. I felt like I was at the funeral for my life as a married person without kids. When I was really worn out and feeling sorry for myself, I felt like our baby girl had stolen my birthday.

In *The Baby Book*, Dr. Sears says that weeks after the baby is born when you find yourself wild-eyed and haggard, stomping around your apartment saying you don't have time for a shower because "the baby NEEDS me," the right answer is, "The baby needs a healthy, happy, rested parent." In other words, don't push your limits.

That Saturday at the nature park, we found our limits.

I think it was a good idea to get away for a few days before the baby was born. I wouldn't change that. But the trip felt like detox. I felt like we had been bleached.

The problem was in all the romance of thinking about being new parents and the giddiness that made us want to "do something" to make the baby come, we had drained our batteries.

I decided we needed to take it easy. We needed to go for more walks. We needed to read a good book. April needed to take more naps. I don't think we'll go for another hike in the woods anytime soon. That was not a good idea.

Our motto this week has been, "There's nothing else that needs to happen before the baby is born." Our ducks are in a row, which brings us back to bird watching.

We did take a boat ride on the lake. I did have to ask for more directions from a lady hanging up laundry in her front yard, and we did have to walk an unmarked dirt path along a river to get there, but we found it. And when we did, there was this little old man with a fishing boat waiting at the end of the dock. We puttered around the lake, and the little old man threw seed to the birds.

39 WEEKS, 2 DAYS
Nice

Our friend Jitu is in town to give an intercultural seminar at the university. Jitu lives in Madrid, but he visits often, usually to submit paperwork for his visa or knock the dust off some books at the university library, and he always stays with us. I think it's safe to say we're a little protective of our time with Jitu. Not like we tether him to the coffee table or anything, but we like having him in our home. It's possible we've started nesting early.

Okay, and I would be lying if I said it didn't have anything to do with his cooking. Every time he stays with us he makes chicken curry and chapati bread for lunch. We sit and eat all afternoon.

So this Wednesday when Jitu came to Castellón, he made arrangements to stay somewhere else. He was being considerate, so I didn't complain. I mean I wouldn't stay with someone five days before her due date either—except for my sister, actually. I did do that. But I didn't know what I was doing at the time.

Besides, we're probably a little moody too, like astronauts would be five days before launch date. We know as well as everyone else does that when this baby is born we will be jettisoned into a whole new life like we've landed on the moon.

Still, I'm getting a little sick of people being considerate. I'm tired of being self-absorbed. I don't like the fact that each day feels like a mental game of Jenga. And I wish I had the energy to actually do one nice thing for somebody.

So after the intercultural seminar, I was standing with Jitu in the hallway, and I felt the sudden urge to shed my pregnancy skin and do something nice.

"Come and have dinner at my house tonight," I said to Jitu. I wasn't asking a question.

"No, no," Jitu said politely. He's Asian. He knows how to say no nicely.

"No, really" I said. "I want you to come to our house tonight."

Jitu laughed nervously, probably wondering why I looked so serious, and probably not quite sure what to do about that. Should he honor my wishes or send me home for bed rest?

Jitu thought for a moment, then grinned.

"We'll stop by the grocery store," he said, "and we'll make Indian food for you at your place tonight."

He seemed pleased with this compromise.

"No," I said, shaking my head thoughtfully, "I want to make dinner for you."

"We'll just stop by the grocery store..." Jitu repeated, not quite sure why I wasn't listening to him.

"I'll make chili," I said. "An American specialty for my friend from India."

I smiled and sighed with relief.

It wasn't going to be easy, but one way or another, I was going to do something nice.

39 WEEKS, 5 DAYS
Due Date

What are most couples doing the week of their due date if they are not having a baby? The answer is absolutely nothing out of the ordinary.

My cell phone rang this afternoon, so I answered it.

"Kelly?"

"Yes," I said. It was Encarna.

"Damián called earlier this afternoon, and you didn't answer the phone," she said. She sounded hurt.

How could I have played with her emotions this way? We could have been at the hospital having a baby for all she knew.

I've gotten into the habit this week of including in the subject line of my emails something like "no baby yet, this is just a normal email" to put everyone at ease.

Having a baby will be exciting, but it's not exciting yet. There's nothing to talk about, and nothing to do, except wait. And waiting by definition is the absence of doing anything at all. In fact, the curious thing about waiting is that if you try to turn it into something to do, something active, time actually slows down. It freezes up. I'm pretty sure Einstein references this in his theory of relativity.

"A watched pot never boils," they say, and the more I think about the baby coming, the more my life begins to feel like a space montage from *2001: A Space Odyssey*, one of the most slow moving films in cinematic history. It's actually not half bad if you watch it in fast forward.

So, even though today is two days before our due date, I got up and went to work like any other day. It was the best thing I could do. Unfortunately, the only real news I have to tell you is that things are about as normal and uneventful as possible. April and I are just sitting here twiddling our thumbs.

In fact, I'm quite sure Troy, our friend and colleague in Madrid, experienced the most boring phone call of his life this morning.

"Hi, this is Troy," he said.

"Hi Troy," I said.

"How are you?"

"Good."

"What are you up to?"

"Working."

"Any contractions yet?"

"Nope."

"Anything else that might possibly make this phone conversation more interesting?"

"Nothing to speak of."

"Hmmm....."

Okay, so Troy didn't say that last part, but he probably got off the phone and yawned.

So, what I can tell you is I'm going to bed now. Tomorrow

I'll get up, and I'll go to work again. And maybe, just maybe, we'll have a baby tomorrow. Now that would be exciting!

39 WEEKS, 6 DAYS, 5:13 AM

Contractions

April woke me early in the morning and told me her contractions had started. I jumped out of bed—Clark Kent, looking for the nearest phone booth.

After April convinced me to sit back down on the bed, she explained that I had already slept through hours of her lying awake trying to decide if the pain in her hip sockets meant today would be the day our baby was born.

We sat there wondering until April dozed off. Eventually I climbed back into bed, and we slept until the alarm clock went off.

I've never stopped to think about what heroes do when they're not saving people. I suppose they act like everyone else. Take firemen, for example. When they're not running through flames, they're probably feeding their cats, or jogging, or mowing their lawns. Most of the time, they're ordinary people.

I was ready to be a hero today. No, I had no plans of hacking apart a burning building with an ax, or even chasing a cat out of a tree, but I did want to take care of April while she was in labor.

What I didn't realize was that labor can take a long time, and while April has been in labor all day, there's not much we can do except be patient and carry on with our everyday lives until it's time to go to the hospital.

We went out for lunch to celebrate that April is in labor. Afterwards, April curled up on the couch with a book and fell asleep. There wasn't much else I could do, so I did what I do every other day: I went to work.

39 WEEKS, 6 DAYS, 7:03 PM

Evacuation Plan

We had an evacuation plan. Our suitcase was already sitting at the front door. The stopwatch was on the dresser in our bedroom, and as soon as the contractions were minutes apart, I would call Damián and Encarna to pick us up with their car. In the meantime, I would gather together a few last things like our toothbrushes and April's favorite pillow—all of which I had written down neatly in a list.

At least I thought we were prepared to leave the house until April's water broke. She had been napping on the couch all afternoon, then without warning she sat up and looked around—as if something had changed, she just didn't know what.

We heard a loud snap, like a twig breaking, and April screamed. She ran to the bathroom, and I followed yelling, "What happened? What happened?"

"I don't know. I think my water broke," April said as she sat on the toilet.

The water was gone now, and no thanks to gravity, our little girl was like a bowling ball wedged between April's hips.

The next contraction came, and April didn't know what to do with herself because of the pain. She thrashed around, screaming and puffing air, looking for some way to twist her body to lessen the pain. I felt like I was locked in a room with a wild animal. April was unpredictable and unwilling to listen to me. She was relying on instinct now to guide her, and her body was doing the work. Between contractions, she sat concentrating, her eyes fixed on the floor, her mind behind armor, protecting itself. She was a tank, and I had no way of getting inside.

Watching a person in labor feels like watching someone drown. It's that horrifying. I knew I had to leave April in order to help her or we would never get to the hospital, but I couldn't imagine leaving her there by herself, as desperate as she was to hold my hand. I also knew I needed to think straight for both of us, but my mind was like traffic noise. I couldn't distinguish one thought from another.

After the next contraction passed, I sprinted across the apartment to our bedroom only to discover that I couldn't find my list and the stopwatch was broken, which shouldn't have mattered, actually, because on any other day I would have remembered that if your wife's water breaks, you go to the hospital immediately. You forget about the stopwatch because the baby is coming.

At least Damián and Encarna were on their way. I had called them when April's water broke and told them April was in labor. I said they didn't have to come yet, but to be ready. When I called them back because April's contractions were on top of each other and I wasn't sure what we were going to do if we had to wait for them, Damián said they were only five minutes away. They had hopped in their car the first time I called.

Somehow Damián and Encarna knew more than we did. Maybe it was because they were parents and grandparents, and they had seen this all before. Maybe it was the way close friends know you're in love before you do.

Whatever it was, Damián and Encarna knew something else we didn't—April was much closer to giving birth than we realized—because when April and I finally found ourselves alone in our quiet hospital room, thankful for some peace and quiet, Encarna charged in and demanded to know where the nurses were and why we weren't doing anything about their absence.

Encarna dragged me to the nurses station to show me what it looks like when a person takes control of her own situation. She took one of the nurses by the wrist, led her down the hall, and pointed into our room.

Encarna and I stood by as the nurse put on her rubber glove

and checked how far April was dilated, then calmly walked over to the intercom, pushed the button, and with her back to us, whispered, "We need a doctor immediately. She's a 10."

39 WEEKS, 6 DAYS, 8:27 PM

Delivery Room

The elevator doors opened, and a nurse rolled April into the hallway on a hospital bed. Another nurse pulled me aside, and I watched April disappear through the double doors at the far end of the hallway before I was pushed into an empty room, handed some scrubs, and left alone.

I put on the scrubs, and while I sat waiting for someone to come and tell me what to do next, it dawned on me that the baby could be born while I was waiting in this room. Everyone else had a role to play in order for the baby to be born, including the guy who had rolled April down to the delivery room on a hospital bed. I was the only one who was literally just sitting around waiting for the baby to be born.

I was optional. Having me at the birth was like deciding whether or not to put sauerkraut on your bratwurst. A bratwurst is still a bratwurst, no matter how you dress it. My role was to be a dad, but I couldn't do that until the baby was born, and even then, I was unsure about what I was actually supposed to do.

A nurse popped her head into the room.

"Your wife needs you."

I followed the nurse into the delivery room. I had never been in a delivery room before, and it reminded me of a laboratory, although I had never been in one of those either. It was partly everyone walking around in scrubs and lab coats with shiny instruments. It was also the attitude. Everyone was so deliberate and concentrated on what they were doing, to the point that they seemed oblivious to the woman on the table in the middle of the room with her legs in stirrups. She was the human body, the next lab test. But to me, she was April, my wife.

"Can I push?" April asked when she spotted me at the door.

"I don't know," I said as I ran over to her side.

I looked for the midwife, who frowned and shook her head.

"We'll have to wait for the doctor," I said.

April looked away. Her chest heaved as the tears began to roll down her face and then her neck.

I leaned in and gave her a kiss on the forehead.

"You're doing great," I whispered in her ear.

And that's when it clicked. The job of everyone else in the room was to make sure April delivered a healthy baby, but mine was to be April's husband. The baby was the last step. I wouldn't be a dad until the very end. In the meantime, I was a husband, and that was the one thing that separated me from the rest of these people.

I was the only person in the room who actually knew this woman. It mattered less what I did, and more who I was. I was the guy who seven years before had made a commitment before God to stick with April no matter what life would bring her way, even if that meant being by her side in the delivery room with nothing more profound to say than "You're doing great."

Watching the birth was not what I expected. I was holding April's hand the whole time, so I saw about as much of the actual birth as April did.

Even when our little girl was finally in my arms, I was busy holding her up and trying to get April to smile while they put in her stitches.

PART II
Baby

First Night

I sat on the couch holding my daughter in my arms. April was asleep, the nurses had gone, and for the first time, the two of us were alone.

I was as curious about her as she was about me. I pushed her nose, so I knew what it felt like, and admired her fingernails, thin as paper. Each time her eyes opened was like flowers blooming, and she had these tiny, white dots all over her face like someone had sprinkled her with powdered sugar. I ran my fingers over her head and inspected the places where her head plates came together and the soft spots in between, with the same mindfulness I often used to pick out a good cantaloupe at the fruit shop. Her hair was like cornsilk, and when I leaned in close to listen to her breathe, she sounded like a pug—they snore even when they're awake, and somehow they're still cute.

I looked at the clock and was surprised by how late it was. I had lost all concept of time, thrown it overboard in order to travel lighter. After April's water broke, it didn't matter what happened later, or what had gone before. All that mattered was now.

Finally I was beginning to find my place again, like I was flipping through a book looking for the last page I had read. This chapter was called "First Night" and was the part in the story where we all tried to get some sleep. I wondered if this would be a long chapter.

The nurse had mentioned that I could put our little one in the crib when I wanted to get some sleep. She had pointed at the fiberglass box on wheels parked at the end of April's bed.

I walked over and looked in the box. There was a mattress, not much bigger than a pillow, and crisp, white sheets tucked tightly around the mattress like at a hotel.

I had gotten in trouble earlier by the nurse for leaving the little hat on our baby. I guess newborns only need that little hat on for a couple hours after they're born before their body temperature is the same as ours. April was sleeping with her sheets pulled up around her waist, so I decided our little girl would sleep with sheets too. I pulled down the sheets, laid her in the box, and tucked her in.

I stepped away and watched to see what would happen, which was like watching someone practice judo, in slow motion, backwards. Or possibly like watching a weightless astronaut try to rummage through her space kitchen looking for Doritos. Either way, she seemed too preoccupied with operating her limbs to notice me.

I continued to edge backwards until I nearly fell on the couch. The problem now was I couldn't see her from where I was standing. It didn't occur to me that if I did actually plan on sleeping, I wouldn't *see* her anyway because my eyes would be closed. Nevertheless, I rolled the crib over to the side of the couch before I lay down, took a deep breath, and closed my eyes.

I began hearing things. My daughter sounded like Rick Moranis in *Space Balls* when he drinks his morning coffee through a Darth Vader helmet and chokes. She would gurgle and snort, which was like trying to sleep while someone's vacuuming under your bed. Then I wouldn't hear anything for a while, and I would get even more worried that she had stopped breathing.

Every time I sat up to see if she was okay, she just lay there tangling her limbs like an octopus. She was okay, but I wasn't. I couldn't shake the urge to pick her up out of the crib and lay her next to me on the couch.

I realized at that point that no one was around to tell me I couldn't pick her up. I wasn't babysitting someone else's kid. I was dad. My job was to go with my gut on these kinds of things, even if I didn't know what I was doing and all the other parents in this hospital had their newborn in that fiberglass box. I had to do what I felt was right, and I didn't have to feel bad about it either.

By morning, I hadn't slept much, but I did feel more like a dad. I had spent the night curled up with my little girl on the couch watching her doze and trying to figure her out. It was a new day, and we had a lot of work ahead of us, but at least for now I had learned something useful: I knew I liked her.

1 DAY

Choosing a Name

April has been practically in a coma since last night, except for a few attempts at breastfeeding, and even then she's been dozing off.

I've been trying to call family when I can, and they've all been asking the same questions: what time was our little girl born, how much did she weigh, and what is her name? I don't know the answers to any of these questions. It's like asking someone who just hit the ground after parachuting out of an airplane how fast he was going and what time it was when he landed.

We decided to wait until our little girl was born to choose her name. Almost since the beginning of the pregnancy we were stuck between two names. April had her favorite, and I had mine. Neither of us was willing to give up our name, so we did what all indecisive people do, we decided not to decide. Well, actually, we agreed to wait until we could hold our little girl in our arms, get a good look at her and then, we thought, we would just know.

As for our genius plan, well, let's just say that this morning, roughly 12 hours after our little girl was born, we were even less fit to name a child. April was unconscious, and I was scared stupid. I hadn't showered or fed myself or slept. Asking me to name a child would have been like asking a Japanese game-show contestant to name a child while he was playing soccer in binoculars.

Plus, I know it's going to sound funny, but I felt no need to name out little girl because she already had so many names that fit her so well. I call her "sweetie," "cutie," "hey you," "button nose," "*cariño*," in Spanish, and others. I felt like a real parent using these pet names, like the first time I called April my "girlfriend," it felt like a holy word.

I felt bad for April, though, lying in her hospital bed. Maybe that was her plan all along because I just told her we could use her name. So, if you can imagine our little girl in your arms for a moment, please say your first hello to Alleke Grace Crull. Her name is pronounced Al-ick-ah, and we're calling her Allie for short.

We picked Alleke's name mostly because we liked the sound of it, and we could actually imagine ourselves calling our daughter "Alleke" or "Allie," but also because we met an Aleke once (who spelled her name with only one "L"). She lived in the "Jesus Loves You" building near Central Station in Amsterdam where we were students at the time. We found ourselves sipping tea and nibbling on windmill-shaped *speculaas* cookies in her apartment a few times for no other reason than she had very low standards when it came to who she let into her house. Most of us just wandered in.

April keeps telling everyone that Alleke's name is a family name, which it is, but secretly I think she chose the name because Aleke, the one we met in Amsterdam, was a woman who seemed comfortable in her own skin—what with her short blonde dreadlocks that looked like a plant sitting on her head, and her wry smile.

Alleke's name is an aspiration. As her parents, we hope to raise her to be a woman who is comfortable in her own skin because she knows herself well.

I've already been practicing saying Alleke's name to her this morning so that we can both get used to the sound of it. The more I say Alleke's name, the more it's beginning to feel like a tattoo.

2 DAYS
Seizure

"Can you raise the bed up a little more?" April asked. She didn't look up, but kept her eyes fixed on our little girl in her arms as she shifted her around and tried to find a position where she could be tempted to eat.

Watching April breastfeed was like watching someone learn to drive a stick shift—first hunting around for first gear with the shifter, grinding gears, and finally locking into place only to stomp on the accelerator long enough for the car to lurch forward, hiccup, and die. I thought there was no greater sense of defeat until I saw April trying to convince our daughter to eat.

"How's that?" I asked, raising the bed up to a sitting position with the remote.

April nodded.

I figured April didn't need me watching her, so I busied myself cleaning up the room after our second night in the hospital. I happened to look up and noticed April's eyes were closed and her head had fallen to one side. I was thinking she must have fallen asleep when, without warning, she slumped over.

"April, are you okay?" I asked, walking over.

She didn't respond.

I took her by both shoulders and lifted her upright. To my horror, her eyes had rolled back inside her head, the whites of her eyes glowing. Her whole body began to quake violently, and for a moment, I felt like I was only holding a body, the shell of a person.

"Help," I shouted. "Somebody, help me."

I didn't know how to take the baby, and hold this shuddering body still, and call for help all at once. I pulled the baby onto the bed, lifted her into one arm, and ran for the intercom. I pressed all the buttons repeatedly.

"Help!" I screamed. "My wife is having a seizure!"

"Hello?" someone replied.

"Help me, please!" I cried.

I ran for the bed again as April dove for the floor. I held her there, heaving, then managed to prop her up in her bed with my one free arm.

She lay there, completely still. Then squinted and opened her eyes. She looked around.

"What's wrong?" she asked.

Just then the nurse appeared at the door.

5 DAYS

Baby Blues

April squeezed her eyes shut, the tears glowing in the corners of her eyes from the lamp next to our bed.

"I don't know if she likes me," April said.

She looked down at little Alleke, five days old, laying there on the bed between us and smiled a painful look at this little person who had brought so much mystery into our house as suddenly as a firecracker.

I reached over and held April's arm. She looked tired.

We sat in silence, and I thought about April's last few days. After her seizure, the nurses discovered that April had lost a lot of blood during delivery. April wasn't eating much either, and the end result was she was dangerously low on iron, which explained why she had been mostly unconscious.

The doctors decided to keep April in the hospital for four days, which sounded nice at first since staying at the hospital had been like a hotel with room service, but turned out later to be more like boot camp for April. She worked tirelessly. If she wasn't asleep, she was being told to eat and drink more, or she was swallowing vitamins from a plastic cup, or soaking her stitches in the tub, or changing bandages, or practicing feeding the baby.

We arrived home from the hospital with little Alleke in April's arms and me with our suitcase following behind. Our friend Heather from Madrid had walked home a few hours earlier to get the house in order, and as soon as we walked in the front door, Heather put on her most motherly pose and told April to go to bed.

I think we all thought April needed more rest. When April wasn't doing something, she should sleep. Either Heather or I would take Alleke to the living room, beyond crying distance from our bedroom.

Strangely enough, while I was sitting on our bed watching April cry, I thought of our basil plant on the balcony off the kitchen, which is the sunniest place in our apartment. She had been neglected while we were at the hospital. We had watered her and left her in the sun, but somehow she knew we were gone. Her proud green leaves had gnarled like elderly fingers. She looked more stem than leaf.

What April needed was Alleke, I thought. Alleke made our home smell like fresh basil leaves. Without her, the whole thing seemed mad—too much work and a waste of time.

April needed time to be Alleke's mom—maybe an afternoon

together with just the two of them to nap, cuddle and coo at each other.

April pulled her hair behind her ear and gently rested her hand on Alleke's chest. April smiled again, more tears in her eyes.

"I think we need time to get to know each other," April said.

I reached over Alleke and gave April a kiss on the forehead, then bent down and kissed Alleke's little nose. Without saying a word, I got up and left the room.

7 DAYS

Taming Those Little Fists

By the time the church bells had rung three times last night, April and I, and Alleke of course, had been awake for hours. We sat on the bed trying to speak the same language. April eventually closed her eyes and leaned her head back against the headboard. She was out of ideas.

"Do you want to go for a walk?" I asked finally, bouncing little Alleke in my arms, trying to fool her into thinking her dad was excited about the idea. She squished her face up like a dirty Kleenex and began wailing again.

She seemed so strong then, roaring like a lioness. I wondered if I would be able to outlast her till morning. We walked down the long dark hallway to the living room, leaving April to recharge in the silence of our bedroom.

"I promise I'm listening," I said and kissed Alleke's hot little forehead. "I've got all the time in the world," I added, which was a promise I hoped I wouldn't have to keep.

We walked figure eights around the coffee and dining room tables, and I watched her crying in my arms. There wasn't going to be an easy fix this night. All I could do was watch and pray—and hope she would teach me something I didn't know before.

As time passed, I began to see a pattern I hadn't seen before. Alleke would cry until she simply couldn't anymore, and then she would lay there in complete exhaustion as if she had just finished swimming laps. She would begin dozing off, and her hands would start drifting around like helium balloons. Inevitably, one of her little fists would come floating by her mouth, like a lollipop, and she would lunge for it trying to get a lick before it was gone.

Of course Alleke was never ready for her fist to be gone. She wanted more. So she would cry, and when she would cry, she would wake up, and when she would wake up, the whole process would begin again.

Putting Alleke to sleep was a question of taming those little fists.

Now I knew what I needed to do, but didn't know how to do it. First I tried the obvious. I wrapped her up like a little baby burrito with her tiny fists tucked inside the blanket. She wriggled free. Then I tried gently placing my hand over her chest, so her hands couldn't reach her mouth. She wrinkled her nose and screamed immediately, sending the clear message that babies don't like it either when people tell them what they can and cannot do. Finally, I decided all I could do was charm her. I had to convince her that sleeping was better than sucking on that candy fist of hers. I sang to her. I massaged her legs. I held her in her favorite position—lying chest down in my arms with her face looking outward.

It didn't work. She still cried. We walked more laps.

I don't remember much between 4:30 and 5:30, but in the end, I was lying on the couch with Alleke on my chest. We mutually agreed that we had had enough for one night and it was time to go to sleep. We would pick up where we left off tomorrow night—she screaming and me guessing.

Human

"What do think will happen if I just put her in the crib right now?" I said to April, who was squatting on the floor in her pj's sorting laundry.

April shrugged.

"She doesn't look like she's ready to sleep," I observed.

She wriggled in my hands like a puppy. Her eyes were wide open and alert, something which I've discovered doesn't happen very often in newborns.

I gently lowered her into her into the trunk we had converted into a crib, hoping she wouldn't notice, but expecting she would.

I stepped back and watched. She lay there doing her little baby Pilates routine, snorting as happily as a potbelly pig.

April walked over to the trunk and took a look.

"Maybe she just needs some alone time."

I walked across the hall to the bathroom and brushed my teeth. When I came back to the bedroom, April was in the bed and only the lamp next to the bed was on. I got into bed and lay there for a moment.

"Do you think we can go to sleep with her wide awake like that?" I asked.

"Why not?" April asked.

I reached over and turned off the light. The room went gray, and the trunk was a shadow in the corner. I fought my instincts to get back out of bed and take another look at her. I closed my eyes instead.

I woke up once during the night, and the lamp next to the bed was on again. I looked at the clock. It was 4:27. April's back was to me, and I could hear her talking to Alleke and feeding her.

I closed my eyes again, and this time when I opened them, the room was golden with sunlight. The room was quiet. I looked at the clock again. It said 8:43.

I lay there for a moment, then raised myself up on one elbow and looked over at the trunk. It was empty. I closed my eyes, then remembered something about April feeding Alleke earlier. I turned over and April and Alleke were cuddled up together next to me on the bed.

Not until I had crawled out of bed, taken a shower, and put some jelly on toast did I begin to grasp the miracle that had occurred in my home the night before.

The baby had slept.

Don't get me wrong, Alleke sleeps lots. She sleeps every morning and every afternoon. But she never sleeps when we want her to, never when we want to sleep.

"I'm trying to remember what we did last night," April said to my later in the day. "Maybe we can try to do it again."

We're both optimistic. We'd both like to think there's some clue from last night that we just need to uncover.

Still, deep down, I think what I'm really learning is that Alleke is more like me than I thought. Some days I wake up in the morning ready to sit down at the computer and answer emails. Some days I wake up and press the snooze button. Some days I whistle while I work. Some days I turn off the radio and close the door. And the thing is, I don't know why some days are different than others. They just are.

This sounds ludicrous to me now, but I guess somewhere I got the impression newborns were predictable. They cry because they're a) hungry or b) gassy or c) because they want to be held or d) because maybe they have an ear infection or something. But I'm discovering that sometimes they just cry because they cry. Alleke cries because she's human, just like me, and that's what we do, even if we don't know why.

11 DAYS

No Substitute

My mother-in-law, Rachel, has arrived from Iowa for two weeks to help out. She's already gotten in the habit of cuddling up with Alleke on the couch for an afternoon nap. Needless to say, April and I haven't turned down the offer to sleep in our own bed without interruption.

The first nap Rachel took on the couch with Alleke was also the first time since Alleke was born that she was not in the room sleeping with one of us. I didn't really think about it too much, but the funniest thing happened while we were sleeping.

We fell asleep, and two hours later I woke up. At some point during those two hours, I must have woken up just enough to look around the room for Alleke. In the hospital I had gotten quite used to resting Alleke on my chest all bundled up in a blanket while I slept on the couch. Those were actually my favorite moments with her at the hospital.

In my half asleep half awake state, I must have wanted Alleke to sleep on my chest. I got confused, however, because she wasn't in the room and decided instead to pull our sheet off the bed, roll it up into a baby-sized ball, rest it on my chest, and call it good.

I woke up cradling our bed sheet.

14 DAYS

The Manly Art of Breastfeeding

April's has had this book called *The Womanly Art of Breastfeeding* lying on the coffee table for the last week or so. I haven't touched it. Not because I think the topic of breastfeeding is off limits for dads or that it's repulsive or that there's nothing I can contribute to the conversation since I don't have the right equipment.

The truth is April and I have thought so much about breastfeeding in the last two weeks that I'm ready to spend my time thinking about anything else—even that leaky showerhead in the guest bathroom that's been taunting me for ages. I was hoping the problem would just go away.

Still, I feel compelled to write something about breastfeeding for dads. Not because I'm a qualified parent. You should have seen me give Alleke her first bath! Instead, I'm writing about breastfeeding for dads because I want to do you a favor. I want to give you a heads up. So listen closely.

There will come a time when your wife will be lying there—in my case April was in her hospital bed—with as much ambition as a rug and as much emotional and intellectual stability as a Chihuahua, and in that very special place, she will come to a point of such desperation that she will actually ask you—yes you, someone entirely unqualified—to please say something or do something to make this little creature eat, and believe me, even if you don't have anything brilliant to say, you'll want to say something. Mostly because you're not interested in finding out the consequences if you don't, but also because this is your wife and this is your baby, and if there's any time that you've ever been needed in your life, it's right now.

I had been wondering about breastfeeding for months. I wondered what the big deal was. Why did we spend three childbirth classes on breastfeeding? Why did every baby book have at least one chapter dedicated entirely to breastfeeding? And what's with La Leche League, an entire organization just for breastfeeding moms. It all seemed so over the top.

That is, until that second night at the hospital.

Alleke had been squirming in our arms for hours, from seven

o'clock that evening until two o'clock in the morning, and we were lost for ideas. Our brains were ringing, set off balance by the contrast between our quiet hospital room and the screams of our little girl, which sounded a lot like shattering glass.

We had a hungry baby, and we did not know what to do with her.

At that moment I realized that learning to breastfeed is like that recurring dream where I find myself simply falling from the sky towards earth. I slice through the air like a bullet, the trees and roads and cars on the ground coming too quickly into focus. I realize then that I'm actually holding on to what looks like a parachute—at least I think it's a parachute. It's not on my back, it's in my hands, and I've never parachuted in my life, but I better do something because the seconds are spinning away.

What makes breastfeeding difficult is it happens all at once. The moment your child is born, he or she begins losing weight. You have somewhere between three to five days to teach mom and baby how to connect that breast to that little mouth.

Instinct gets you a long ways, but beyond that, you're on your own. I've never been in a situation where I've seen anyone learn something so complicated so quickly as watching my wife and daughter learn to breastfeed together. Breastfeeding is like renting a stick shift for your family vacation without having ever driven one before and deciding you'll figure out how to work the clutch along the way—while you're winding through the mountains in a national park somewhere.

If I had had the money, I would have given every cent of it to our midwife Carmen to have just stayed there with us, sitting on the end of April's hospital bed, coaching us and stroking Alleke's head with her quieting midwife touch, till we had figured out how to feed our baby. I would have even run home and baked Carmen chocolate chip cookies. That's how much I wanted her to stay with us when she stopped in our room during her hospital rounds.

So what about dad then? Well, for starters, just be there. Quit your job if you have to. Your wife just needs you to sit there on the couch and look helpless.

Believing in miracles helps too. Your wife will tell you breastfeeding the baby is impossible, and she'll give you the baby, and she may even pout or cry or scream, but when the time is right, hand her the baby again. Tell her she's capable and that you love her.

Don't think about the future. Don't beat yourself up by thinking about having this little baby with you tomorrow and the next day and the next day. That's emotional suicide. Just think about now. About what your wife needs now and how to get her to believe she can feed this baby.

And if you can find the courage in yourself to do these things, my friend, you've mastered the manly art of breastfeeding.

18 DAYS

The Umbilical Cord

Alleke's umbilical cord fell off this morning. I opened her diaper, and there it was lying on her belly like a piece of beef jerky.

My first thought was, "What do I do now?" which, by the way, has become standard operating procedure. My second thought was, "This kid's growing as fast as a sea monkey. She's already graduated to full belly-button status."

I wasn't sure what to do with the umbilical cord. Should we celebrate? Or hold a funeral? I was uncertain of the protocol, so I left the whole gooey mess wadded up on the changing table.

Later that afternoon my mother-in-law walked into the living room holding Alleke. She had just finished changing Alleke's diaper.

"Are you going to keep that umbilical cord?" she asked. The repulsed look on her face suggested an answer.

I smiled and bit my lip. "I was thinking about it."

Three days later, and my mother-in-law is no longer here to change diapers. As we speak she's probably sipping a Diet Coke somewhere thousands of miles above the Atlantic Ocean, and Alleke's umbilical cord is still lying like a fossil on the changing table between the baby wipes and the baby lotion. I haven't thrown it away because every time I look at it, I am reminded that our little girl is growing up.

I know the idea is laughable. She's so little. So brand new. Still, every day she changes. I can see it. She's not the baby we brought home from the hospital two weeks ago.

28 DAYS
Afro-Cuban All Stars

This morning I was on the couch writing work emails because I only have a couple days left before I go back to work full-time, and April was out getting her final blood analysis done as part of her post-pregnancy checkup. Meanwhile, Alleke seemed genuinely happy to lie there and let her marble eyes roll around the room.

Eventually, though, our little girl caught on to the fact that no one was particularly in the mood to play with her, so she began whimpering like bad plumbing, the corners of her little mouth turned down in her new—and very effective—pouty face.

I could only take so much of her unhappiness before I was scrolling through our iPod looking for something that might cheer her up. The Afro-Cuban All Stars seemed a festive choice, so I pressed play.

The room filled with old Cuban men singing in unison, a piano hammering out the melody, a string bass running up and down the scales, and Latin horns filling in the rest.

I suppose originally I had hoped the music would distract Alleke enough to keep her mind off the sad truth that her dad has a job and can't always play with her, but what actually happened was quite the opposite.

I walked over to the blanket where Alleke was lying, picked her up, and began dancing (what I thought was) the tango. I was possessed by the music. I had to be since I don't dance, ever. Or maybe I was inspired by fatherhood. Either way, I'm sure we looked as elegant as hippos, but oh did we have fun.

Well, at first I don't think Alleke knew what to make of our dancing. We were spinning around, and we were down low and then up high. We were everywhere. Alleke's little eyes were trying to follow all of it, but lagging seconds behind. She looked serious like she was trying to do math.

Towards the end, however, I got the brilliant idea that she might like to moon walk. I had her little legs in my hands like a fork and a knife, and we started cutting through the air to the beat of the music. She seemed to loosen up a little bit then. She looked mildly amused.

The music swelled, and as the Latin horns brought the song to a punchy end, I dropped to my knees and held Alleke out like Simba for everyone to see. She was, after all, the star of the show. Her back was to me, so I couldn't see what she was doing, but her little legs were spinning happily in the air like Freddy Flintstone's.

I turned her around so I could see what she was doing, and you'll never guess what, she was smiling—at me. Her first real smile.

I gave her a kiss on the nose and told her dad liked that very much.

30 DAYS

Jitu Called

He said he was in town again, and he asked if he could stop by.

"When?" I asked.

"How about right now?" he said.

I hesitated.

"Hold on."

I pressed my hand over the phone receiver.

"Who is it?" April asked, nursing Alleke in our green armchair on the other side of the living room.

"It's Jitu. He's in town, and he's wondering if he can stop by."

"When?" April asked.

"Now," I said.

April looked at Alleke for a moment, and then looked back at me.

"I don't know what to say," April said. "She's going to be a while."

What April meant was she didn't want an audience while she was still figuring out how to breastfeed, and Alleke sometimes took over an hour to eat.

I put the phone back to my ear.

"Alleke's eating right now," I said. "Do you have time later?"

"I can change a few things around," Jitu said. "Does seven o'clock work?"

"That's perfect," I said.

I've always wanted a friend like Jitu, by the way. He just shows up at our front door. He surprises us like rainbows do. I love the spontaneity of the whole thing. Plus, we always have meaningful conversations. We don't just fill in the gaps from the last time we talked. We bare our souls. Talking to Jitu is like free therapy. I think it's safe to say friends like Jitu don't come around that often.

I decided to call Jitu back and ask him if he wanted to go for a walk. Usually he comes over to our place, and if I'm lucky, we talk while he makes Indian curry. Lately, however, I've developed an evening habit of taking Alleke for a walk because it gives April a break from both of us and it is the only way I know to consistently keep Alleke happy—although I still wouldn't bet chapati bread on it.

I thought I would try to kill two birds with one stone. Even though by the time we exchanged phone calls and met up two hours later I knew Alleke would be hungry again soon, I still wanted to meet Jitu and give April some time for herself.

We walked and talked. Jitu talked mostly, and I let him because it felt good to listen to someone talk about anything but babies. I could tell Jitu had been waiting to tell me his story. It was a very important one. He was very serious about the whole thing, and when he got to the most important part, we decided to sit down on a park bench in Ribalta Park, the one where the old guys play bocce ball in the afternoons.

Jitu finished his story and took a deep breath.

"So what do you think?" he asked, looking me in the eyes.

I leaned back in the park bench and waited for the carrousel of thoughts spinning in my head to come to a stop. Our conversations often came to a place like this one where one of us would give the other permission to speak into his life. This was a fragile place, and the way forward was a delicate one, like making our way across a lake covered in a thin layer of ice. I wanted to say a few things, and I wanted to ask questions too, and I wanted us to take our time.

Just as I had decided where I wanted to begin, I heard something. It sounded like ice cracking. Then I felt the little head against my chest begin to turn from side to side, trying to work itself free like a cork from a wine bottle.

I looked down into the shadowy baby carrier, and I could see those little eyes pinched together. Her legs started spinning like she was riding a bike, and then came the crying. She whistled like a teakettle.

Jitu looked worried. I'm guessing he was disappointed too. I was. Our conversation was caving in.

Alleke howled like a wolverine. Jitu stood up.

"Is she okay?" he asked.

"Yes, she's fine," I said as I rocked her back and forth in the carrier.

"Maybe she's uncomfortable," Jitu offered. He peered hesitantly into the carrier.

"No, she's hungry," I said. "I better go."

"Right," Jitu added and nodded his head.

Alleke sounded more like a bobcat now. She sounded like white noise, and I even found myself wanting to cover my ears and squint.

"I better go," I repeated. I was getting a little worried now. I was a twenty-minute walk from home.

"Okay," Jitu said. "I guess we'll talk later then?" He was trying to salvage the debris.

"Yes, later," I said, trying to smile. I waved and walked off, leaving him there under the palm trees.

1 MONTH

Tag Team

Today was my first full day back at work. I had been coming in half days for the last two weeks, which meant I had been working just enough to file all my emails for later.

As one would expect after returning to work from a paternity leave, I had an ambitious work deadline to meet by the end of the day. On a good pre-baby day I would have needed a full day to complete the office work I had to do. The difference was today I had a crying baby in my arms.

April had dropped into bed the night before like a bear going into hibernation, and I knew it would be best for everyone if she got some sleep. Yesterday had been a long day. We got up early and took the train to Valencia to apply for Alleke's passport at the American Consulate. By the time we got home I think all of us felt like we had been through shock therapy.

This morning April fed Alleke first thing when she woke up, and then April went back to bed. I wanted to let her sleep until around eleven. Still, I had to figure out some way to be a dad and sit in my office chair.

All I can say is if anyone got an email from me today that was either short, angry or didn't make any sense, the reason is because I had a baby yelling at me. I don't know how Alleke knows, but she knows when I'm not giving her my full attention. She knows if I'm trying to read a book over her shoulder. She knows if I'm putting her down to check email. She knows when my heart isn't in it. She's like a natural parent rating system, and this morning my ratings were going through the floor.

I gave up on sitting in my office chair eventually, after I had worked off every calorie in my body to keep her mildly satisfied. I even gave her a bath in the kitchen sink to keep things interesting.

When April woke up, I handed Alleke off and disappeared into my office. I worked wildly. I sat hunched over my keyboard with the same stoic expression as a church organist. I did not have fun.

In the late afternoon I took a break and found April a mess. She had been trying to feed Alleke all afternoon, but Alleke wouldn't have it. She wasn't interested.

April handed Alleke to me and told me to do something with her. She didn't look like she cared what.

I took Alleke for a walk. I enjoyed that part of the day very much. Alleke clutching my shirt with her little fists as we walked through the orange groves to the basilica and back.

We got home and April fed Alleke while I made dinner. I ate my dinner, then took Alleke while April ate her dinner and talked with our travel agent on the phone about buying plane tickets to Iowa for the end of the month. We were sticking to our plan to move to Iowa for four months to be close to family, and then move back to Madrid. April hung up the phone and took Alleke, so I could sit down on the couch with my laptop.

I'm still working, and now it's late. The room is dark except for one small lamp glowing across the room. I can see the silhouette of April sitting in her chair. She is asleep. Her head is slouched awkwardly against the left side of the armchair. Alleke stirs in her lap, her little fist making a circle in the air and then resting on her cheek, and she sleeps again. I sigh as I realize that I didn't like today very much.

April and I were tag-team parenting. There was no point during the day when we were both in the ring. If one of us was taking care of Alleke, the other person was doing something else. April was doing her thing, and I was doing my thing. We weren't parenting together. I don't know how we'll do things differently tomorrow, but still, today felt wrong.

1 MONTH, 4 DAYS
Choice

Going back to work as a new dad is like being told you're the only one in the office who has to work on Thanksgiving Day. Going to work wouldn't be different than any other workday except that you know everyone else is at home with their families licking gravy off their fingers and dozing off in their La-Z-Boys during the football game.

I wanted to be with my family, not at work, and the worst part for me was April and Alleke were in the next room. I could hear them being family while I sat in my office chair and answered emails and made phone calls and shuffled paperwork. I was being constantly reminded that I could not be with them.

Still, as much as I wanted to be with my family, I was also incredibly relieved to be at work again. The truth is my job is easier than being a father. I know what I'm supposed to do when I sit down in my office chair, and maybe I'm self-deceived, but I think I'm good at my job too.

Being a parent is much less certain. I never know what I'm supposed to do. I don't get much sleep. And when I'm holding Alleke, I can't do anything else. Sometimes I feel stuck or I get bored. There are days when I'd rather stay in the office than walk into the living room and be a dad.

In some ways the first weeks were easier because I had to be a dad. April was slow to recover and slept almost as much as Alleke did. While April slept, I had to figure out how to hold my daughter and change her dirty diapers and survive sleepless nights.

Alleke was experiencing our world for the first time, and I felt very much the same. I was experiencing our world as a dad for the first time. It was just the two of us, and even though neither of us had much experience with being a daughter or a dad, we made it work because we had to.

Now, the challenge has changed. I'm not as necessary as I once was. I'm one of two parents, and I'm the one with the job. Someone will change Alleke's diaper if I don't. Someone will feed her if I don't. Someone will give her a bath. But, I'm choosing to show up and be her dad. I'm going to pull my weight not because I have to, but because I want to.

These days love is a choice.

Plastic Cup

Yesterday I fed Alleke for the first time. April even let me sit in her special breastfeeding chair, the green one. I cradled Alleke in my arms, and she licked breast milk out of a little plastic cup that I had taken from the top of a cough medicine bottle.

April and I decided I should feed Alleke from a little cup because Alleke is underweight. At our first check-up at the hospital, the pediatrician who looked young enough that I'm convinced he still lives with his parents told us we should give Alleke a bottle because breastfeeding wasn't enough. I can't think of an insult that would make April more furious, and I could hardly keep up with her as she marched home and pounded out an email to the folks at La Leche League. They suggested feeding Alleke from a little cup and weighing her every day to see if her growth rate improves.

The first time I fed Alleke she was all smiles. She licked happily from the little cup, and her tiny fist held tightly to my t-shirt. She cried when she was finished, and I rocked her to sleep.

The second time I sat down in the green chair to feed Alleke, she would not have it. She was hot and angry and glowed like embers. Her fists swung at the little cup in my hands. I managed to feed her a few milliliters, but when I sat her up to see if she had swallowed them, they bubbled out of her mouth like soap suds.

When she finished yelling at me, she fell asleep, her small arm hanging awkwardly over mine like a dead branch.

All the while April was busy on the couch hiding her smile in a pile of paperwork.

"Are you laughing at me?" I asked.

April bit her lip.

"No," she said and shook her head innocently.

"I got her to sleep, didn't I?" I said.

April smiled and shrugged her shoulders.

"Well, we're going to take a nap," I said.

This was my trump card. I had gotten her to fall asleep. Surely I could get her to take a nap. April was in the habit of taking a nap with Alleke every day at this time, so I figured we would do the same.

We walked to the bedroom. I slid off my slippers at the foot of the bed, pulled off the covers, and climbed into bed. I laid Alleke down next to me, all bundled up like an Eskimo in her blanket.

I took my eyes off her for a second to reach for the covers. I looked back to see if she was asleep, and there she was, completely still, both eyes wide open and looking at the ceiling.

I leaned over and placed my hand on her chest.

"Alleke, it's time for a nap," I whispered.

She carefully turned her head to look at me with those wide eyes. She looked very serious, her forehead all bunched up, and then began to cry.

Alleke and I still don't speak the same language, but I knew what she was saying.

"I want my mommy."

1 MONTH, 13 DAYS
Radio Wave

"Babies don't grow in a straight line," the pediatrician said. He clicked his pen and drew a straight line at a forty-five degree angle on a piece of hospital stationary.

"Babies grow more like this." He drew another line. This one looked squiggly like a radio wave.

He smiled. "Alleke's going to be just fine," he said. "Just give her time."

I believed him right then. Maybe because this pediatrician looked older and wiser than the first one. Maybe because I needed someone to tell me Alleke was going to be okay. Or maybe because I knew that if someone had charted out my mental health over the last two weeks, it would have looked a lot like that squiggly line on the piece of paper. Still, somehow I knew things were going to be okay for all of us in the long run.

Our lives were a mess right now, moving boxes literally everywhere and trash bags waiting at the front door, but I knew from experience that sometimes things can get a little crazy and erratic, but as long as we were headed in the right direction, that's what mattered.

The pediatrician handed us the little orange book that had Alleke's medical records in it. As we left the hospital, I flipped to the page where the nurse had written in Alleke's weight and charted it on a graph. Her weight looked a lot like a radio wave. It looked chaotic. I looked at the dates and did the math. Alleke had grown more in the last week than most babies do in two.

She was headed in the right direction.

1 MONTH, 18 DAYS
Moving Day

Yesterday was our moving day. Apparently many of our neighbors also had this day marked on their calendars because while I was carrying boxes out to the truck, they were busy as bees blowing up bouncy castles in our square, blocking off the streets with metal gates and constructing a small stage. They even carried in armloads of dry firewood which they dropped in metal cans and lit on fire to warm giant cast-iron skillets for making paella.

In the evening marching bands roamed the streets, firecrackers erupted from every corner of the city, and fathers and sons ran through the square blowing fire at the crowds.

I couldn't help thinking that somehow the city of Castellón was saying its farewell to our family. Our plan was to leave in the morning for Madrid where we would catch a flight to Omaha. My parents would pick us up from the airport and drive us back to Iowa.

Alleke and I woke up early. I put a hat on her head, bundled her up in a blanket, and we closed the door of the apartment behind us quietly as we ventured out into the streets to see if there was anything left of the colorful weekend in the city.

We sifted the streets with our neighbors and followed the thin blue line that ran crookedly through the streets. Eventually we were overtaken by a stampede of gangly marathon runners, so we stepped onto the curb and watched them pass.

To my surprise, the street filled with smiles. Many of the tired runners grinned, even waved at Alleke, as if she were their patroness spurring them on to the finish line. She was as much a weekend attraction as the runners themselves.

In the street on the way back to our apartment, an old couple was setting up a food stand. They both smiled and the old woman hurried around the table to get a look at the little baby I had bundled up in my baby carrier. I bent down so she could take a look at Alleke who was now sound asleep with her face looking straight up into the sunshine.

"Oh, that's too cute," the old woman said and waving over her husband.

He left what he was doing, walked over, and both of them peered into the carrier.

"How old is she?" she asked.

"Six weeks," I said.

She shook her head.

"Well, stop by again soon," she said and smiled at me.

I smiled back.

Later in the morning I brought our friend Shani to the train station while April fed Alleke at home. Shani had come for the weekend from Madrid to help us put all our things in moving boxes.

As I walked home, I passed the old couple at the food stand. The old woman was talking with friends and serving them giant donut holes with tongs from a pot of boiling oil. Her husband sat reading the paper in a folding chair with his feet up.

I watched the old woman, hoping I might catch her attention and say hello. Our eyes met briefly, and I smiled, flashing my hand in her direction.

"Hi again," I said.

She lifted her chin and squinted at me for a moment. Then, without a flicker of recognition, returned to her conversation. She had dismissed me, I suppose, as someone who had wrongly mistaken her for someone I knew.

I walked the rest of the way home, marveling at how easily I had forgotten that without a little baby, I was just a stranger walking down the street.

1 MONTH, 19 DAYS
Getting from Point A to Point B

I suppose I didn't help things when I told the taxi driver it was his fault we were going to miss our train. Yes, that comment might have been unnecessary. Although I wasn't exaggerating. I knew the taxi service in Castellón was bad, but not this bad.

I wished we had learned this lesson on any other day than

the one we were leaving town, the one where we were standing on the curb with all nine of our bags and a baby waiting for an unfriendly man to bring us to the train station so we could make it official that we had missed our train.

Handing the taxi driver our biggest bag first hadn't helped either. He grabbed the bag with both hands, hoisted it onto the bumper of his car, and nearly tumbled into the trunk with the bag before he got it where he wanted it.

He came out of the trunk with a red face.

He swore, looked at the rest of our bags, and told us this was not normal.

"It's not actually your fault," I said—an apology, sort of.

The taxi driver smirked, as if to say, "Tell me something I don't know."

"It's just that I called for a taxi three times, and you were the first one to come," I continued. "If we don't get to the train station in the next ten minutes, we'll miss our train."

The taxi driver shook his head.

"I can't take all these bags," he said.

"We called for two taxis," I reminded him.

The taxi driver looked down the street and laughed.

"Can we fit these bags?" I asked, rolling two more suitcases over to the back of the taxi.

"One more," he said, holding up his hand.

I lifted the bigger bag into the back of the car and the taxi driver closed the trunk. He walked around the far side of the car and got in.

April rubbed my back briefly and looked me in the eyes.

"I'll be okay," I said. "I'll see you at the station."

April climbed in the back of the taxi with Alleke asleep against her chest in the baby carrier, and the taxi sped away.

I arrived at the train station a full half an hour after our train had left for Madrid. I left most of our luggage on the curb, lifted one of the hiker's backpacks onto my shoulder and walked into the train station.

April was at the top of the escalator, sitting on one of our suitcases, another one sitting next to her, and Alleke still asleep against her chest in the baby carrier.

April didn't say anything about missing the train, and I didn't say anything about why I had taken another half an hour to get to the station. I suppose we understood it was in our best interest to look forward, not backward at this point. We needed to get to Madrid, tonight.

We had three options: train, bus or car.

The car was at the bottom of our list. Neither of us had ever driven a car in Spain in the four years we had lived here, let alone paid attention to how it was done. We did have our U.S. driver's licenses, which meant the people behind the desk at the car rental place on the far side of the train station would give us keys to a car. We had had enough adventure for one day, however, and the goal was to keep things simple. We would take the train.

Before I handed my credit card to the man behind the ticket window, however, I asked about our baggage allowance. He said each passenger was allowed fifty pounds. It wasn't until the next day that I actually weighed our luggage and discovered that our bags weighed only a little less than three hundred and thirty pounds, but I knew enough to smile and walk away.

We only entertained the idea of the bus for a few moments before we remembered that we were no longer the young, spontaneous married couple without kids. We now had a baby.

Sure, she looked small, but she was as loud as a foghorn. Even if we could make it to Madrid without setting her off, I didn't want to. I'd be wound up as tight as a ukulele all five hours.

Which left us jingling the keys to a small Seat Ibiza. I think the woman at the car rental place may have questioned my driving ability when I told her we were going to Madrid, then added as an after thought, oh yeah, do you have a map, because I don't actually know how to get there. Although, by the looks of her map, she must not have been too concerned. Her map was three dots connected by two lines. Castellón was the first dot, Valencia was the second dot, and Madrid was the third dot. I just had to connect the dots.

By the time we were on the road, it was already getting dark. I had to pull over to find out how to turn on the lights. We found the highway, then realized we didn't know the speed limit. We buzzed along for fifteen minutes, no road signs with numbers of any kind, before we decided to call Troy who drives. He said I should drive 120 kilometers an hour. I sped up a little bit.

The idea was to stay over night at Troy and Heather's house in Madrid. I told Troy I didn't know what time we would arrive because I didn't even know where I was. I told him I'd need directions to his place. He started telling me about this highway and that exit, and I realized this was going to be complicated.

"Look," I said, "Why don't I call you back when we get closer. I'm not going to remember any of this anyway."

I hung up the phone and handed it to April. She looked at it.

"Your phone just died," she said.

"What?" I said.

I took my eyes off the road for a second to look at the phone. We sat in silence.

April's phone hadn't had credit for days, so we had been using mine. Now we had no way of calling anyone, including Troy.

I guess for now all we could do was follow the big green signs, like the one we had just passed, that said, "Madrid, 367 km."

I learned something about the human spirit on this trip. I learned that when our options are whittled away to almost nothing, we are capable of all kinds of things we never would have imagined.

I never imagined mouthing off to a Spanish taxi driver, for one. Or renting a car and driving half way across the country when I didn't even know the speed limit or how to get where I was going. I never imagined I would have to slip into the bathroom in a Spanish bar and search around the toilet for an outlet so I could plug in my phone and call Troy to ask for directions to his house.

Furthermore, when we boarded the plane in London, and I checked the digital screen in front of my seat, and the estimated flight time to Chicago was not six hours, which I was planning on, but eight, and then when the plane sat on the runway for another hour, I didn't think I was capable of the journey ahead, not with an infant.

I didn't know if any of the passengers were going to make it, actually. We were all stuck on plane with a baby. She was only six weeks old, and as such, still undomesticated. She was a wild creature. As her parents, we mostly still followed her rules and instincts, and to date I had never known her to sit quietly for nine hours—or six for that matter—without howling.

Of course I don't think anyone would blame a baby for crying. We all know crying is the way babies get their point across. An adult might ask, "May I please have a nice tall glass of milk?"

Alleke, in contrast, screeches like a parakeet. It's just the way it works.

Still, patience on airplanes is a prized commodity. While I've discovered that some of Alleke's cries are actually nicer than others, I'm sure to everyone else they all sound like a band saw.

I wish I could tell you we made it to Chicago without Alleke crying, but that wouldn't be the truth. What we did discover, however, was that one loud noise cancels out another. When Alleke would get gas and start to squirm on my lap, I'd strap her into the carrier and head to the back of the plane where the engines hummed like vacuum cleaners. Alleke would yank at my shirt with her fists and scream until she felt better. I watched her like a silent movie.

I suppose we were so relieved to be in Chicago that we weren't fazed by the fact that we had less than one hour to go through customs, pick up our luggage, check in our luggage, transfer to another terminal by shuttle, go through security, and run to our gate to make our flight to Omaha. I don't think we felt particularly lucky that we were two of the last four people to get on the plane before they closed the door behind us. We just felt tired.

We arrived at Omaha at ten o'clock at night. April wore Alleke in the baby carrier, and I carried the diaper bag and two backpacks to the baggage claim area.

My parents were waiting for us there. They were about to meet their granddaughter for the first time.

April sat down on a bench, reached behind her neck and unclipped the baby carrier, then gently lowered Alleke into her lap. Alleke's face and sleeper were wet with milk. Her hair was matted against the side of her head on one side, and it stuck out like feathers on the other. She smelled sour.

Then, slowly, without a care in the world, she stretched, lifting her fists over her head like a kitten, as she always does, and as if on cue, looked at Grandma and smiled.

We had come all this way, and in that one brief moment, we knew our journey had been worth the trouble.

1 MONTH, 27 DAYS

The Common Cold

I was beginning to think Alleke was immune to all earthly diseases.

First she survived three plane cabins and their recirculated air on the trip to Omaha. Then we drove to Iowa to celebrate Thanksgiving Day with both sides of the family, and Alleke got passed around from Grandma to aunt to niece to Mom to Dad to uncle to niece to aunt to Grandma and back again.

Most of us got sick. Uncle Rick got bronchitis. April got the head flu. Cousin Emma got a rash. Aunt Sherri got violently ill with the flu that everyone around town was talking about.

Alleke got hugged and kissed and held and touched with sticky fingers and sweated on, and she survived it all.

What can I say? She's built to last.

Then, just when no one was sick, Alleke got her first little baby booger. I could see it hanging there like a spider in her nose, and I grabbed it with a Kleenex. (I don't like spiders very much.)

The next day Alleke began to cough. She wheezed like a squeak toy. Her nose ran like glue. April and I wondered what we should do. Our baby was sick for the first time, and all we wanted to do was do something. Anything.

I go to the doctor almost every year for bronchitis. It's an annual tradition. The first thing most doctors say is, "Get some rest and drink lots of water." The problem in Alleke's case was we were already doing those things. Alleke had made an occupation out of sleeping and eating, and she was still sick. There wasn't anything else we could do—except, of course, worry over her and make up reasons why she was sick.

That's why I spent yesterday afternoon moving boxes out of my old bedroom in my parents' house. Alleke sleeps in this room with us, and it's dusty in there. The room is literally piled full of boxes of stuff we left behind when we moved to Spain. Walking into that room is like walking into someone's past—oversized suitcases, knit blankets, model cars, board games, paintings in frames, pottery, shelves of books purchased from Goodwill, old T-shirts, pots and pans, a Chinese wok, abandoned guitars, the list goes on. I carried all of these things from the bedroom into the family room and stacked them against two walls. I filled half the living room with our stuff.

My mom vacuumed the room when I finished.

We thought Alleke might be allergic to the dust. We didn't know for sure—it was a theory—but we couldn't handle the thought of all that dust in there once the idea settled in our heads.

This is the life of a new parent. We make decisions based on very little information and even less experience.

2 MONTHS

Boogie Boogie

If you change a lot of diapers, it helps to be funny.

Or at least it helps if you have an act. I imagine if you asked most parents how they spend their time at the changing table, they wouldn't tell you about baby wipes or diaper rash, they would tell you about their variety show, about how they've learned to juggle toilet paper rolls or dance the tango with the plunger or sing opera into a tube of toothpaste. Changing diapers is less waste management and more stand-up comedy.

Let's face it, the actual job of changing one diaper for another is about as exciting as licking stamps. Babies learn this as quickly as parents do. They don't need to know what we know—that we'll change their diapers some 5,000 times before they even reach the age of two. They know changing diapers is boring business. And so, our babies train us to entertain them.

The reason I mention any of this is because last week at the changing table I discovered Alleke had refined her sense of humor. She now knows what she thinks is funny. Smiling at her, tickling her feet, and blowing on her tummy always work, but as for jokes, well...

I had growled at Alleke like a closet monster, giggled like Winnie the Pooh, even made my fish face. These were our jokes, and none of them seemed to be working. Alleke yawned, studied the plaid curtain hanging in front of the water heater, and tried to put her whole fist in her mouth.

"Oh yeah," I said, "Well, at least I don't have a booger hanging out of my nose."

I leaned over until my face was in her face.

"Boogie boogie," I said.

Alleke lifted her eyebrows and looked at me.

"Boogie boogie" I said again.

She took her fist out of her mouth and kicked her feet.

"Boogie boogie," I said.

She shook her head and opened her mouth wide.

"Boogie boogie" I said, laughing this time.

Alleke scrunched up her nose and giggled.

I picked Alleke up off the changing table and kissed her forehead.

"Do you want me to say it again?" I asked.

I looked her in the eyes.

She stared at me, all serious, then reached for my nose.

Anniversary

"That reminds me, we still haven't figured out what we're going to do for our anniversary," I said.

April had the TV on, and she was feeding Alleke on the couch. She looked at me, but didn't say anything.

"I'm just saying, every time I bring up our anniversary you want to talk about it later, and the 18th is two weeks from today."

"I'm not reluctant," April said, setting the record straight.

"Okay, here's what we can do," she said. "Either we go to Sioux Falls for the day and take Alleke with us, or we give Alleke a bottle and get a babysitter so we can eat at the Pizza Ranch in town."

She lifted Alleke onto her lap and began patting her back.

"What do you think?" she asked.

I laid my head back in my chair and looked at the TV. I liked both of April's ideas. They were the kinds of things we would have done for our anniversary the last six years of our marriage. But I could tell that what April was really saying was that whatever we did, we were going to have to work for it. Romance was not cheap these days.

A trip to Sioux Falls meant more than an hour each way with a screaming baby in a car seat, changing diapers in public restrooms, breastfeeding at a restaurant, and altogether missing the point that we meant to have a night for just the two of us.

Eating at the Pizza Ranch in town meant teaching Alleke to take a bottle in the next two weeks so we could leave her with Grandma or Aunt Heidi. Somehow bottle feeding seemed more overwhelming because then we had a deadline for teaching Alleke something we had never done before and had no idea how to go about.

I looked at April again. She was waiting for me to say

something. I smiled an apology and wished I hadn't brought up our anniversary.

2 MONTHS, 4 DAYS

Little Miss Sunshine

I have been begging April to watch a movie with me for weeks. Tonight the social orbits of the seven people who live in April's parents' house aligned perfectly so that April and I were home alone with Alleke asleep in April's arms in the rocking chair. I grabbed my coat, crashed through the front door of the house, and sped off in the family minivan to Mr. Movies on the other side of town.

I arrived back at the house with a copy of *Little Miss Sunshine* only to find my mother-in-law watching TV in the living room by herself. She took her eyes off the TV long enough to tell me that April had gone to bed with Alleke.

Two days later I returned the movie without watching it.

"We need to talk," I said to April this afternoon and convinced her to go for a walk with me. We hadn't talked in a week. Before we even left the driveway we were already arguing. I wasn't surprised since we had learned from the beginning of our marriage that if we were arguing that usually meant we hadn't been spending enough time together, which was exactly my point.

Alleke was a slow eater. Some babies take minutes to breastfeed, but Alleke often took two to three hours, which meant April and Alleke sat in the rocking chair most of the day. We had also decided that we didn't want Alleke to cry herself to sleep, which meant if April wasn't in the rocking chair, she was napping with Alleke in our bed. When April was up and about, I was expected to take care of Alleke so that April could have time for herself.

As we walked across town with the snow crunching under our boots, and Alleke warm against my chest napping in the baby carrier under my coat, I explained to April that I felt like this little person was controlling our lives. I understood the importance of listening to Alleke's cues so that she knew she could trust us to meet her basic needs, but what about my needs? Was I selfish for wanting my wife to pay attention to me?

April got defensive. "What do you want me to do?" she asked. "Let Alleke cry when she's hungry so I can pay attention to you. She's a baby, Kelly, and you're an adult. Her needs come first."

We walked in silence for a while, listening again to the snow under our feet.

"I was just surprised by how quickly you shifted your priority from me to her," I said quietly. "It seemed so easy for you." I stopped and looked April in the eyes.

"Don't you miss me?" I asked.

April stared at me and didn't say anything.

I sighed. "I don't trust you right now," I said. "I don't believe that you would put me first if I asked you to." I felt the tears burning around the edges of my eyes as I realized that I believed what I had just said. "Most couples say they're going to put their kids first, and twenty years later they wake up in an empty house and realize they don't know each other anymore. Unless we take the time now to understand our relationship to each other, I'm scared I'll lose you."

2 MONTHS, 5 DAYS

Bounce

One of the first habits I made after Alleke was born was bouncing with the baby. Alleke liked to keep things moving, so I got in the habit of bobbing up and down to a steady rhythm. It didn't matter if we were waiting in line at the grocery store, or standing at the stove over a skillet of onions and garlic, or watching the big game on TV, we were always moving. Strapping Alleke to my chest in the baby carrier was like setting her on the washing machine and pressing the "Start" button.

Two months later, however, I have to admit things have gotten a little out of hand. I've learned that good habits become bad habits when I'm still doing them even after they serve no real purpose.

April and I had been invited to speak in a class at Dordt College, our alma mater. This class happened to be the largest one on campus. We were standing next to the professor listening attentively as he introduced us, and that's when I noticed April had Alleke in the baby carrier, but I was the one bouncing. We had been in front of the class for minutes, and I had no recollection of how long I had been dancing my own groove.

Of course I stopped immediately and sort of tried to hide behind April for a while, and when the professor finally walked away and left us standing there, I half expected someone in the back of the room to yell, "Giddy up!"

All week I've been trying to find the courage to tell April about my problem and to ask for help. Finally, this morning, when April walked into the kitchen and pulled the Crispix out of the cupboard, I confessed everything. I even told her about the college class.

"I know," April said, not looking at me as she filled her bowl with cereal. "You were bouncing just now when I walked in the kitchen."

2 MONTHS, 7 DAYS

Women's Coat

I pulled April's coat out of the closet at her grandma's house. I looked at it and shook my head. It was a long woman's coat with big brown buttons on the front and a bow on the back.

April was right. I did want to wear Alleke in the baby carrier on our walk back to her parents' house where we were staying now. She was also right that it was a good idea for me to wear a long coat that I could pull over Alleke so her little toes wouldn't get cold. What I wasn't sure about was whether it was a good idea for me to walk across town in a woman's coat wearing a baby.

In theory, I had always thought fanny packs were a good idea too, but that didn't mean I was actually going to wear one. I stood at the door for a minute looking the coat over while April's uncles and aunts and cousins chatted over pie and ice cream in the living room. Finally, I decided maybe wearing a women's coat wouldn't be that bad. I pulled the coat on and fastened all the buttons.

"Why don't you take Alleke outside and walk around," April said. "Maybe she'll fall asleep."

"Alright" I said.

"I'll be out in a few minutes," April added as I opened the door and walked out into the snow.

I walked up the road a ways, bouncing Alleke, and she fell asleep. I began walking back towards the house, and I saw April coming out of the garage and pulling on her mittens.

I stopped and waved.

April covered her mouth with her mitten, then threw her head back and began to laugh.

"You look pregnant," she yelled, walking towards me, "and with your long hair, you totally look the part." She laughed some more.

When she got to where I was standing, she gave me a kiss on the cheek. "Now I know why everyone inside was watching you from the window."

She smiled, took my hand in hers, and tugged me in the direction of her parents' house.

2 MONTHS, 12 DAYS
Movie Theater

"Two tickets for *The Pursuit of Happyness*," April said. She handed her card to the high school kid behind the counter, and while the machine printed our tickets, April took my hand in hers.

"Enjoy the show," the kid said as he handed April the tickets and her card.

"Thanks," we said and walked in, following the overhead signs to our theater. We pulled open the door and disappeared into the darkness. Inside, we whispered.

"We're the only ones here," I said, looking around.

The theater was a small black box. The screen was miniature, and as we stood at the entrance and watched a preview of falcons chasing children through an animated forest, I felt more like we were looking through a window into a theatrical world than stepping into it. I had no intentions of complaining, however. We were on a date, and we had this small black box all to ourselves.

April smiled and pulled me by the hand up the stairs.

"Where do you want to sit?" I asked.

"Right there," April said and pointed at two seats in the center of the middle row.

We sat down, took off our coats, and the movie began. The story with Will Smith and his son unfolded before our eyes, and as we sat watching, my arm around April, I couldn't help feeling like we were old friends reunited. Since Alleke was born, we had learned quickly to recognize each other as mom and dad, but we hadn't been these two people for a while, the ones cuddled up in a movie theater. When I thought about these two, I usually thought about the past.

We watched more of the movie, and Will Smith had a title for each chapter of his life. One was called "paying taxes," and another one "running," and still another "internship." I wondered what I would call this chapter of my life. I thought I might call it "dad," but I wished it would be something different, something more. I wished April and I could figure out how to be mom and dad and husband and wife at the same time. I missed being the couple in the movie theater.

That's when April surprised me. She mixed our worlds together as casually as if she were stirring milk into her coffee. In one instant, she was both mom and wife.

She ran her fingers through my hair, then leaned over and whispered in my ear.

"Do you think I can pump milk here?" she asked.

We had left Alleke home with Grandma, and because April would normally feed Alleke right now, she had to pump milk instead. That's how breastfeeding worked.

I smiled.

"You know you're crazy," I said, scanning the theater again. "But I don't see why not."

I shrugged my shoulders. "We're the only ones here."

April grinned, then kissed me on cheek.

"Good," she said, "Then I can stay here with you."

2 MONTHS, 16 DAYS
Fire Drill

I stepped into the house from the garage and stomped the snow off my shoes. I hung up my coat and walked into the kitchen.

On the counter was an open box of cereal. The milk jug was there too and the carton of orange juice along with a soggy bowl of cereal with a spoon in it. The house was quiet.

April didn't finish her breakfast again, I thought. She must be feeding Alleke in bed.

The life of a new parent is one fire drill after another. I have to be willing to stop whatever I'm doing at the moment and do something else. I don't often get to do what I want to do when I want to do it—at least not for very long. Life is cut up into small pieces.

I'm not very good at fire drills. I like finishing one thing before I start the next. I eat my lunch one food at a time. I read books one book at a time. I write stories one story at a time. At parties I prefer to talk to one person at a time.

I've always admired secretaries, like the one at the clinic where April had her pregnancy check-ups, who could talk to someone on the phone and jot down notes while waving us over to the counter to take our insurance card, and afterwards, pick up on a conversation she was having with one of the other secretaries about where they should go for lunch.

If someone gives me information over the phone, I ask him or her to wait while I write the information down.

On bad days I feel discouraged that so many people can do what I can't. They can stop what they're doing and do something else. On good days, however, I see each fire drill as an opportunity to grow up a little bit and become more of the person Jesus is teaching me to be. In the meantime, April and I are just trying to finish our bowls of cereal.

2 MONTHS, 18 DAYS

Cliché

Last night I tried putting Alleke in the baby carrier with her face forward. She's just tall enough now for her eyes and nose to peek out the front. She looked like a little ninja master with the bottom half of her face masked behind the black fabric of the carrier. While I was walking around the kitchen making tuna salad, April said Alleke's little eyeballs were bouncing around in her head like lottery balls because she was trying to take everything in so fast.

Alleke didn't last long, though, before she began meowing like a kitten. I was in the middle of squeezing the water out of the tuna can into the kitchen sink, so I asked April what I could use to distract Alleke for a few minutes while I finished making dinner.

"She watches TV," April said, looking up from her laptop. I followed April's line of sight to the small TV sitting on the kitchen counter next to the sink.

"I don't want her to watch TV," I said, offended.

April shrugged her shoulders, as if to say, "You asked," and began typing again at her computer.

I didn't think TV would be a big part of Alleke's life. I guess I thought we would be one of those families that played board games and read literature and baked cookies and practiced the alphabet. I thought we might even floss our teeth before we went to bed.

The truth was I had been giddy with excitement the night before when April came home with *X-men 3*. Alleke had sat quietly on my lap, her two eyes drawn to the TV like magnets. The screen had beamed with laser light, flickered with bolts of lightning, and splintered to pieces as rock-solid mutants rammed through prison walls like armored tanks. The surround-sound speakers in the corners of the room had squealed with tearing metal, jolted with machine gun fire, and exploded as the mutants collided in civil war on Alcatraz Island.

Alleke had watched it all, amazed.

I'm pretty sure Alleke would have had a chance at a life without much TV except for one small truth. I'm Alleke's dad, and I like watching TV. And I have a hunch that parents who watch TV have kids who watch TV. I was living out the greatest parenting cliché of all time: one parent trying to fulfill his dreams through his child. I secretly wanted Alleke to be everything I thought I should be.

I wish I read more books. I really do. So badly in fact that I went to college and got a degree in books. I still like to buy books, but then I end up watching TV while the books sit on the shelf.

I don't think it matters if I'm talking about not wanting Alleke to watch a lot of TV or not wanting her to be shy because I was the kid who hid behind my mom's pant leg. The issue is it's unfair to ask Alleke to be the person I wish I was. I keep trying to remind myself that Alleke will make her own decisions. The ones I can control are my own.

2 MONTHS, 19 DAYS
Lost in Yonkers

The usher showed us to our seats. We took off our coats and put them on the backs of our chairs.

"Good seats," I said as I looked around. Our seats were in the second row. What I meant, though, was that our seats were at the end of the row and near the exit.

April opened the program, and I read over her shoulder. The play was called *Lost in Yonkers*. The audience hushed, and the lights went down. Two shadowy figures moved across the stage and took their positions.

With one hand, I held April's hand in mine, our fingers mingled. In the other, I held the cell phone I had borrowed from Grandma. I pressed a button on the phone, and the screen lit up. No missed calls.

2 MONTHS, 20 DAYS

Nightlight

I don't remember exactly what April and I talked about last night in the glow of the nightlight. I do remember somewhere towards the end, just before we fell asleep, turning over so I could see April, or at least her silhouette, and asking her what it would take to wake up in the morning and feel like a good dad.

We had talked for a while about being a mom and a dad and how we both loved our daughter, even more than we had expected, just like everyone had said, and that even though we were beginners and didn't know much about parenting, we both felt capable and excited to learn with Alleke as she grew. I told April I loved watching her be a mom, I was thankful we had a good marriage, and despite a few hiccups along the way, I felt like we were on the same page.

That's about the time I asked April the question, the one about wanting to wake up in the morning and feel like a good dad. Because even though we both felt like we had so many good things going for us, there were still some days that we felt like bad parents, like we were raising Alleke all wrong. In fact, the more we talked about it, the more we realized that we felt this way most of the time.

We speculated about why we felt like bad parents, which wasn't so hard to do at a quarter past eleven when we were exhausted from another long day and felt incapable of most things, including the present conversation, but April came up with something profound, as she usually does. She said, "I mostly feel like a bad mom when I feel like I'm supposed to want to be with Alleke every minute of every day, and...I don't."

That was it.

We loved Alleke. We even loved being with her most of the time. We just didn't want to be with her all the time.

I still woke up this morning feeling like I was supposed to want to be with Alleke all the time, but I felt a little less bad about being her dad. I think what changed was I stopped to realize that I don't like being around anybody all the time, not even April. What helped even more was realizing that even though Alleke is great, she is a lot of work. She wears us out, and sometimes we just need a break. Everybody does.

So at around four this afternoon I handed Alleke off to her Aunt Heidi—who took her even though she was crying—and I took my laptop downstairs so I could have some time for myself and write these words.

2 MONTHS, 22 DAYS
Cousins

Marrying April is one of the smartest things I've ever done—of course because she's a great listener, she's intelligent, she's got a cute squishy nose, and she loves me, but also because my wife happens to be cousins with half my high school graduating class.

We are from Iowa after all, where there are more cows than people. So for those who have never thought about the advantages of living in a place where youngsters have to ask mom if they're cousins with so-and-so before asking him or her on a date, consider this: when I married April, five of my best friends became my cousins.

Needless to say, this year I was looking forward to Christmas in Iowa because of the sheer efficiency of it. I would go to one family gathering and see many of my best friends.

This particular family gathering happened to be on Monday, Christmas Day, which was at the end of one long string of Christmas gatherings. We began on Friday night with an intimate gathering with most of my immediate family. Saturday we added my brother, my grandma and the cousins. Sunday we spent the day with April's immediate family. Which brings us back to Monday, Christmas Day, the day to see best friends.

April and I woke up tired on Monday morning. We had had lots of help with Alleke over the weekend. Lots of our little nieces and nephews who wanted to hold Alleke. But we were also new parents, and this was our first Christmas as a family, and we had spent the whole weekend never quite knowing what to do with ourselves. We had been fidgety.

By Monday morning we were disheveled, and our breakfast conversation was sour. We agreed, however, to make the best of our day. We live in Spain, after all, and this was our one chance to see lots of best friends. We would not be tired.

At noon we drove over to our college campus. One of the dorms was just big enough to hold April's extended family—her grandma, sixteen aunts and uncles, thirty cousins, four first cousins once removed, two turtledoves, and a partridge in a pear tree.

Most of the family had not met Alleke yet, so when we walked in, the building hummed like a beehive.

"We've got her," one of April's aunts said as she took Alleke from my arms. "Go get yourself some food." And that was it. I was free to go.

I put some food on a plate, poured myself a glass of apple cider, and found a seat at a table with Kevin and Andy, both friends and cousins. We began talking about work and play and everything in between, and I felt like we had never been apart. I definitely didn't feel like I lived an ocean away, which was nice for a change.

Not much later, however, I realized I was still tired, which was confirmed soon after by one of the aunts who stopped by and told me so. More cousins with plates of food joined us at our table, and our conversation sped off in another direction, leaving me behind, grinding my gears, trying to get my head to shift into second gear.

My emotions took the wheel, and we bumbled off the road into the ditch—our wheels spinning in the prairie grass.

I heard Alleke crying across the room and recognized the opportunity to use my daughter as an excuse to retreat to the hallway. In a matter of minutes I found myself out of the picture. I had Alleke in my arms, her head nestled up under my chin, and we were walking up and down the empty hallway while I sang Christmas carols softly in her ear.

I took a deep breath. I felt much better. Still, I wanted to be honest with myself about why I was here in the hallway. It wasn't about Alleke. It was about me, about being tired and needing some space.

Babies learn quickly, but so do parents. Soon after Alleke was born I realized she was my ticket out of everything I didn't want to do. Alleke was my excuse to stay home. Alleke was my excuse to be late. Alleke was my excuse to watch lots of TV.

Yes, I was tired. I was a new parent. I had a good excuse. But, some of my best friends were in the building, and I was hiding out in the hallway.

I have to admit I'm still bitter (often) with Jesus about the amount of growing up I've had to do in such a short amount of time. Regardless, I got my act together. I changed Alleke's diaper, handed her off to an aunt, refilled my cup of apple cider, and sat back down at the table with my cousins.

3 MONTHS, 8 DAYS
Share

I've been talking to a shrink. There, I said it.

After my argument with April when I returned *Little Miss Sunshine* without watching it, I decided that my anniversary present to April would be me signing up for a few counseling sessions. How romantic, right?

When we lived in Madrid I always encouraged others to see a shrink if their problem was beyond my expertise as a pastor, but when the time came for me to make the same choice, I would have much rather taken my wife out to dinner at a fancy restaurant for our anniversary. When I called Mike for an appointment, I had a hard time even explaining why I had called.

I was hesitant to talk openly at first since I didn't know Mike personally, and at one point in the first session when he actually asked me, "How does that make you feel?" I rolled my eyes.

Mike has helped me, though, to understand my situation and explain it more clearly than I would have been able to myself, so let's see if I can share what I've learned.

I've appreciated April's effort over the last month to prioritize our relationship. She took me to the movies and to a play. We've been going for walks, and we're having sex again (which is a whole other story). Still, I feel lonely. Our relationship will never be the same again, and April is not as available as she used to be. We're no longer a couple, we're a family. There are three of us, which means less time for each of us.

While April and Alleke spend lots of time together breastfeeding, napping, and playing, I am on my own a lot more often than before. To be honest, at times I feel like I've lost my best friend. While April has been eager to get to know her little girl, I've grieved the passing of a special season in our marriage where we always had time for each other.

What helps me is to remember why April and I wanted to have kids in the first place. We wanted to share our lives with someone. In hindsight, I don't think I'm very good at sharing, or more specifically, I don't think I'm very good at sharing April. But I'm learning to share, which is one of life's simplest lessons—one we teach to even the youngest of children—because after all, true love is giving someone else what you love most.

3 MONTHS, 15 DAYS

Sex

Nobody told me my wife wouldn't want to have sex with me after the baby was born.

I'm not talking about the first six weeks. I expected that. April needed plenty of time to recover, and we were all busy making faces at the baby. But when we finally found our rhythm, and it didn't include sex, I realized something had changed.

As I tried to articulate to April my frustration, confusion, and insecurity, I found myself asking a good question: what is sex for? I wondered what we were missing without it. If sex were merely a recreational activity, like playing racquetball, I could live without it. There were lots of things we used to do for fun that were no longer compatible with our lifestyle, like staying out late with friends or going away for a romantic weekend. For the most part, we had given up these things and found new ways to have fun.

With some soul searching, I discovered that sex was more than a recreational activity, it was a form of intimacy. What was actually at stake was not fun, but feeling wanted and valued as April's husband and best friend. I missed being the focus of her attention, delighting in each other, and practicing trust.

Apparently many women lose interest in sex after the baby comes along. It's partly biology. Hormonal changes during breastfeeding can decrease sex drive. Probably more helpful for me as a husband, however, has been simply taking the time to put myself in April's shoes and consider whether I would still be in the mood if I was exhausted, in need of a shower, and experiencing high levels of stress or depression—all at the same time. I imagine it's like trying to pee when someone is watching.

By listening to April, I've also learned that while for me sex is a *means* to intimacy, for her sex is an *expression* of intimacy. In other words, for me intimacy is the result of sex. For April, it is the complete opposite. Sex is the result of intimacy.

Like many parents, we've decided to schedule a time in our week for sex. This helps both of us, and accounts for our differences. For me, if I don't feel like April is paying much attention to me, at least I know there will be time for intimacy later in the week. For April, she has time to prepare herself and to let me demonstrate—using other forms of intimacy—that I care about her and value her friendship so that she's ready to express our intimacy through sex.

Honestly, the whole experience has been painful at times. I didn't think it was possible for April to show so little interest in me, even for only a short time. On the other hand, the absence of sex is what as driven me, perhaps out of desperation, to find out what sex is for. I know more now than I knew before about my relationship with April, and so I can say without hesitation that I have no regrets.

3 MONTHS, 24 DAYS
Don't Be Such a Baby

My older brother Chad and his wife and three kids live about an hour's drive from my parents' house, where we're staying again. We had pizza at Chad's house this evening, and on the way home, when the inside of the van was dark as a theater and Alleke was strapped into her car seat like a roller coaster, I noticed then that Alleke was leaking raw sewage out of her diaper. I rummaged through the diaper bag only to discover that we had no diapers, no wipes, and no extra clothes. We would have to wait until we got back to my parents' house to change Alleke's diaper.

When my dad pulled into the garage, I was tempted to grab the garden hose and hose Alleke off, but instead I carried her at arm's length upstairs to the bathroom where I got my first good look at her. She looked like she had been playing mud volleyball. I took my time taking off her diaper, her clothes, and then scrubbing her down in the bathtub.

All the while Alleke was smiling at me. She didn't seem concerned at all. A few times she got bored, so she kept herself busy by either putting her whole fists in her mouth or testing out her voice by squealing at the top of her lungs.

In the end, I was convinced that babies are some of the most accommodating, understanding, and patient creatures on our planet. I don't think any one of us really wants their job, and I would go so far as to say that none of us could stand having their job for a minute.

Let's consider for a moment, shall we?

Babies eat the same food every day. They don't get to pick out their clothes or decorate their rooms. They don't choose their friends or babysitters or even who will kiss them or hug them or hold them. It doesn't make much difference to anyone if they don't like someone's perfume. Most of the time they're told when to sleep and when to play, when to be quiet and when to smile and do their tricks. They have to wait around for someone to cut their nails or blow their nose or change their diaper or give them a bath. They can't itch their elbow or stop someone from tickling their feet, and no one seems to speak their language, at least not without a heavy accent.

I remember this story about Jesus where all these parents were bringing their sick babies to him hoping he might be able to help them. Jesus' friends started shooing the parents away, but Jesus called them back. "Leave these kids alone," he said. "Don't ever get between them and me. In fact, if you never learn how to approach life with the simplicity of a child, you'll never get it."

Maybe the process of growing up is not what we thought it was. We think of adulthood as the goal. With age, we become better people, more sophisticated and complete. Instead, maybe adulthood is, in actuality, the slow process of losing the very virtues we had hoped to attain with age.

3 MONTHS, 30 DAYS
Shots

Alleke discovered a new emotion today.
Fear.

While April filled out a form for a nurse sitting at a card table with a laptop, I took a seat on one of the plastic chairs lining the wall, put Alleke on my knee, and looked around. The traveling clinic was set up in one large open room. A little boy in a diaper sat on his mom's lap in the opposite corner as two nurses on either side of him swabbed his thighs.

One of the nurses noticed me watching with Alleke. She smiled, then pulled a curtain in front of the little boy and his mom so we couldn't see each other. I listened as one of the nurses behind the curtain counted to three, and then the room was silent. The little boy gasped for breath until the air stuck in his chest, and he began shrieking hysterically. He wouldn't stop.

Alleke looked at me. Her smile turned up side down, her eyebrows wedged between her eyes, and she also began to cry. She sat there studying my face, and I knew what she wanted.

She wanted me to make everything okay. I watched the tears pool in the corners of her eyes and run down her cheeks.

I stood up and looked around. I saw a window in the hallway, so we walked over to it. I held Alleke up to the window and pointed at the cars going by on the street below. Alleke smiled, her cheeks shining like polished silver. I kissed her on the forehead, and we watched more cars.

I could hear the nurses talking in the room behind me. They counted and the room was quiet again. The silence stung in my ears, and before the little boy even began to cry, Alleke's face was twisted up and she was looking at me again and crying.

I held her close. There was nothing else I could do. She was next in line, and neither of us was ready to sit in that chair.

April came to the doorway.

"What's wrong?" she asked.

I looked at Alleke.

"She's scared," I said.

4 MONTHS, 6 DAYS

Panic

We all have panic attacks. Which of us hasn't checked our pockets for our wallets when we've left the front door or double-checked the times on our tickets at the airport or wondered whether we've left the water running or the door unlocked or the window open or the stove on. Which of us hasn't walked into a public bathroom and wondered whether we walked into the wrong one, the one of the opposite sex.

I've done all of these things, more than once. Still, I've never panicked as much as after Alleke was born. She worries me. I wasn't worried that she would get sick or that we would hurt her or that she would scream for the rest of her life. Instead,

I kept things simple and worried about one thing. I worried Alleke would stop breathing.

Yesterday April was speaking about our life in Spain at a weekly women's group called Coffee Break. The group meets at a church, so while April was speaking, I wandered around the building and kept Alleke asleep by swinging her in her car seat.

The pastor of the church was in his office, so I stopped to chat. We got talking about globalization and other things, and I completely lost track of time.

At some point I realized I had forgotten about Alleke. Although I was still swinging her with one arm, I hadn't thought about her for a very long time. Alleke was hidden under a blanket, and I hadn't heard a peep from her in over three hours.

I panicked, and I wondered if she was still breathing.

I pulled the blanket off her and set it on the floor. She didn't move. I held my finger under her nose to see if I could feel warm air. I couldn't.

I apologized. "Sorry," I said, "I'm a new parent. I just realized I haven't checked on my daughter for a while, and I'm worried."

I bent over the car seat and listened for Alleke breathing. I couldn't hear anything.

At that point I felt less foolish and more worried. I felt sick instantly.

I shook Alleke's arm, and she didn't move. I lifted her eyelid with my thumb, and she just lay there. I sat back on my knees, took a deep breath, and pulled my hair out of my face.

"I don't know why she won't wake up," I said, looking at Alleke.

"I'm sure she's okay," the pastor said as he knelt down next to us.

I reached into the car seat and carefully, but quickly, lifted Alleke out and removed her snowsuit. I held her in my arms.

The copy machine chirped from the room next door. Alleke

stirred. Then she startled. She flinched every time she heard the sound, and she began to cry.

I held her close, then looked at the pastor and smiled.

For a moment, I felt as if my daughter's life had been spared. She had been pried free from the jaws of death, and now, she was safe in my arms. Soon, however, I realized where I was. I was on my knees in an office cradling my daughter in my arms with a man I had just met who was probably wondering what just happened.

I felt foolish once more, and wondered why I had woken my sleeping baby from a good nap.

4 MONTHS, 9 DAYS
The Public Bathroom

"Did you see a changing table in the women's bathroom?" April asked.

"No, no changing table," April's grandma said. She pursed her lips together in an apology. "But it seemed clean enough," she added.

April's grandma had carpooled up to the Twin Cities with us for a few days to visit her other grandchildren, and now we were on our way back to Iowa. We were making our customary stop at Erbert & Gerbert's Subs & Clubs for lunch in Saint Peter.

"I guess I'll have to change Alleke's diaper on my lap," April said. She took one more bite of her sandwich and set it aside.

"I can do it," I said.

April hesitated. "Okay," she said.

I gulped the rest of my water, then reached for the diaper bag.

"Okay, what do I do?"

April raised her eyebrows.

"I mean, what do I do if there's no changing table?" I asked as I lifted Alleke into my arms.

"Well," April said. "You sit down in the bathroom, you put Alleke on your lap, and you change her diaper."

"I have to sit down?" I asked, grimacing.

April smiled.

"Oh, and I would put down that water-resistant mat we have in the diaper bag," April added. "You don't want her to pee on you. We still have three more hours in the car."

I shook my head and walked off to the bathroom.

The bathroom was one small room, a cube, with a toilet and a sink. It looked clean enough, but looks don't tell you much in a public bathroom, especially when you're contemplating sitting on the floor.

The floor looked about the same everywhere—well, at least everywhere I looked. In better judgment, I chose not to look behind the toilet or under the sink. I decided on a spot close to the door because it was as far away from the toilet as I could get, which in actuality, wasn't that far.

I didn't want to touch the floor with my hands, so instead, I pressed my back against the wall and slowly lowered Alleke and myself to the floor. The experience felt a bit like repelling off the side of a rock face for the first time—slow and steady, fully aware of what awaits below if anything goes wrong.

We got settled on the floor alright, considering the circumstances, and with a little extra care, I managed to change Alleke's diaper without dropping anything on the floor and keeping Alleke entertained.

"We did it," I said as we walked up to the table where April and her grandma were waiting with their coats on.

"She didn't cry," I said, "and neither did I."

We walked to the car, and I told them the whole story. I finished as we pulled onto the highway.

Grandma was holding her book on her lap, and she looked at me.

"Maybe next time," she said, "you could put down the lid on the toilet and sit there while you change Alleke."

She paused.

"Instead of sitting on the floor," she added.

She smiled, thoughtfully, then opened her book and began to read.

4 MONTHS, 24 DAYS

Total Immersion

Putting a baby to sleep is like learning Spanish. I only do it when I have to.

I'd like to say I speak Spanish for the love of the language, but in reality, even though we'll be moving back to Madrid soon, I haven't spoken a word these last four months in Iowa.

Knowing this about myself, last year when we chose to stay in Spain for Alleke's birth, in part it was to put ourselves into a position where we would have to learn the language. We had no other option than to go to a Spanish doctor, enroll in Spanish childbirth classes, and spend many hours at home learning the vocabulary we would need to communicate in the delivery room. We thought about asking one of our bilingual friends to translate for us in the delivery room, but we took the risk and decided not to as a way of challenging ourselves to use our Spanish even in a very important moment in our lives.

We learned Spanish in that situation not only because we wanted to, but also because we put ourselves in the situation where we needed to. Simply put, I've discovered that I don't do even the things I want to do if I don't have to do them.

Now, you may be wondering how learning Spanish relates

to putting a baby to sleep. Well, about a month ago April asked me if I would learn to put Alleke to sleep. April wanted to go shopping and then out for dinner with her mom and sister, but she was stuck at home until I learned to put Alleke to sleep.

Originally April put Alleke to sleep every night because Alleke nursed to sleep. These days, however, Alleke didn't want to nurse to sleep anymore, so as long as she had been fed recently, theoretically I could put her to sleep.

In actuality, I didn't have much to learn. I had to read Alleke a story, sing her a lullaby, and rock her to sleep. Alleke's routine was as straightforward as making Macaroni and Cheese out of a box. I simply needed to follow instructions.

The days went by, however, and I found myself making up excuses why April should put Alleke to sleep and not me. I was tired because I had been working all day—as if April hadn't been working just as hard or harder than me. April was faster at putting Alleke to sleep than me, so the sooner April put her to sleep, the sooner we could have time for the two of us. I even told myself it was better for Alleke if April put her to sleep. Alleke was tired, and I would keep her up late trying to learn to put her to sleep.

A week and a half went by. Each night I made another excuse why I shouldn't learn to put Alleke to sleep. I wondered why I wasn't willing to try. Eventually, one night April and I went for a walk and talked about how I wasn't doing what I had said I would do. I think I was actually more upset about the situation than she was because I didn't like the thought of saying I would do something and then not doing it. I realized as we talked that I had made putting Alleke to sleep much harder than it had to be. The problem was simple: I knew April would always be there to put Alleke to sleep if I couldn't, so I couldn't. I wanted to learn, but I didn't need to.

So, I told April the only way I was going to learn was if she decided to go away one night and left me home to fend for myself. If I needed to put Alleke to sleep by myself, I would figure it out somehow.

The next day April left the house for a few hours to work on her Masters thesis. Alleke got tired, so I decided to try to put her to sleep. Nobody else was around, so I pretended I knew what I was doing, and I rocked her to sleep.

They say babies know when you're nervous. I'm sure Alleke knew I was nervous, and that's probably why she went to sleep so easily. She knew I needed chances. She woke up a half an hour later, even though she normally sleeps an hour in the morning, but I didn't care. I had put her to sleep all by myself.

So here we are almost a month later, and at night April and I take turns putting Alleke to sleep and putting her back to sleep if she wakes up. I really don't mind doing it anymore.

Now, if I can just learn Spanish before Alleke does.

5 MONTHS, 9 DAYS

Grandpa

"I can babysit," my dad said.

April stopped reading the paper and looked up at me. I glanced from her to my mom who was standing in front of the open refrigerator, milk in hand, staring at the two of us. We all looked back at Dad.

"You'd have to change her diaper" April said.

Dad guffawed and looked at Mom.

See, my dad doesn't do diapers. I ask him all the time just for fun if he'll change Alleke's diaper, and he just laughs and shakes his head.

My dad is a good grandpa. He spends lots of time with his grandchildren, and he loves them. But my dad is not a mechanic.

When a little one spits up or smells funny or begins to cry, my dad hands baby off to my mom for a tune up.

Until today, that is.

"I can change a diaper," Dad said, shrugging his shoulders.

I smiled.

I smiled because he was willing to try, and I smiled because he didn't know how.

"Let me show you how to change a diaper," I said.

I took Alleke, and Dad followed me downstairs. I showed him how to change a diaper, then gave him a few tips on how to put Alleke to sleep for her evening nap. We went back upstairs, and April gave him a crash course on feeding Alleke from a bottle.

I told Dad we had the cell phone if he needed us for anything. We kissed Alleke goodbye and left. I was still smiling when we pulled out of the evergreen trees onto the gravel road and headed for town. We would be moving back to Madrid in five days. Dad wanted to give us one last opportunity for free babysitting before we moved away from family. I wasn't sure how long Dad would last with Alleke, but I had to let him try.

I used to think moms had super powers. I even thought April had super powers at first. I thought maybe she was engineered to take care of kids better than I was.

I've changed my mind, though. I don't think you need super powers to take care of a kid. You just have to be willing to do it, and you have to pay attention.

I didn't know much about Alleke when she was born. I didn't know how to hold her, what clothes to put on her, when or how to feed her, or even how to change her diaper. I wanted her to stay alive, though, so I watched April closely and I asked lots of questions. I read books. I watched others. I called my sister. I searched the Internet.

We've developed so much material about Alleke over the last

five months, I could write a user's manual—one with lots of pages and diagrams and fine print. No hocus-pocus. Just how things work. Cause and effect.

For example, when Alleke arches her back, she's hungry. When she rubs her eyes, she's tired. If she shivers, she probably has a wet diaper. And if you sit her up and help her focus on something in front of her like a rattle, she can sit up by herself for almost ten minutes.

My dad doesn't know most of these tricks, but neither did I when I first met Alleke. Every one of us has to start at the beginning at some point.

There are others who are more qualified in the mechanics to take care of Alleke than my dad, but if he was willing, I was going to let him try.

5 MONTHS, 18 DAYS

Jet Lag

I looked at the clock. 2:04 AM. We were in Spain, I was in bed, and it was the middle of the night.

My mind was like a scratched CD, playing the same fragments of thought over and over again in my head.

For the moment, my mind was busy scribbling Spanish on a white board. I was practicing what I would say to Alex, our new landlord, mentally rubbing out words with my fingers, and writing in a better Spanish word until I had a few sentences I liked. If everything went well, tomorrow morning we would sign our contract, and Alex would give us the keys to our new apartment.

I was supposed to be sleeping. I rolled over and looked at April. I could see the whites of her eyes glowing from the light shining into the room from the hallway. I wondered how long she had been awake.

Alleke lay next to her, turned inward, one fist resting on April's chest, holding her shirt.

"She's better at this than we are," April whispered in my direction.

I nodded into my pillow.

Alleke hadn't seemed to mind being in Omaha, Chicago, London and Madrid all in one day. She had kept to her normal nap routine and rubbed her eyes to tell us when she was tired. She even got most of a full night of sleep, despite being in mom's arms on the airplane, in the baby carrier with dad at the airport, buckled into a car seat as we buzzed around Madrid, and finally in bed in the guest room where we are staying until we move into our own place, at which point we'll probably buy a mattress and camp out until the moving truck arrives.

We all went to bed on Spain time. April and I wondered if Alleke would sleep. She was on an American schedule. We were too, but we had done this before. We had our tricks. We had stayed awake during the day by getting lots of sunlight, taking a long walk, and keeping ourselves busy unpacking our bags.

In the end, we went to bed tired, but never fell asleep. Alleke just went to sleep—as if it were simply a matter of setting her clock ahead seven hours.

Tomorrow morning Alleke will wake up ready to play, and we will be zombies.

5 MONTHS, 19 DAYS
Sick

I lay on the mattress on the floor in our apartment and watched April as she rung out a soapy rag and wiped down the empty closet on the far side of the room.

Alleke was sitting behind me on the mattress. I had my back

turned to her because I was trying to get some sleep. I reached my arm over the side of the mattress and felt around for the box of kleenexes. I found it, pulled out a tissue, and blew my nose.

Alleke started to cry. She cries louder now, more like a demanding little girl than a baby, but it was worse today because my head was full. Alleke screamed again, and my head stung.

April turned around and looked at Alleke, then she looked at me.

"Give her the blanket," April said, nodding.

I turned over and pulled the blanket up next to Alleke. She grabbed it with her fists and put it in her mouth, then she looked at me and giggled.

I smiled and dropped my head back in my pillow.

Worse than a sore throat, a cough, and a leaky nose was the guilt I felt for leaving April to take care of herself, Alleke and me, as well as clean the house before the moving truck would arrive tomorrow with all our things, all because I was sick and couldn't get out of bed.

I'm fascinated by how closely connected our mental and physical parts are. When, for example, we're stressed about something (a mental process), it helps to go for a run (a physical process).

When, say, in the last week you have put yourself through the stress of moving back to Spain, living with friends in Madrid till you find an apartment, moving into the apartment, then waiting for the truck to show up with all your things the following day, and your body tells you it's all just too much (a mental process), I can tell you from experience, the result is that you get sick (a physical process).

My body hit its limit, and like a natural circuit breaker, blew a fuse. I had to slow down and take some time to rest and get perspective.

I used to think this was helpful, you know, after exams or acting in a play or meeting a big work deadline. Sometimes I got sick after these highly stressful situations were over, and I knew my body was telling me to take it easy. This time, however, it's different. I'm a parent, and when I get sick, April has to take care of everything.

At the end of the day, I told April I was sorry I was sick and that she had to be in charge of everything, including cleaning the apartment. She just shrugged and said it was fine. I felt worse. I guess because I wasn't sure I could do the same for her.

5 MONTHS, 23 DAYS
On Strike

Alleke screamed again. She arched her back and tried to get away from me. I held on to her tightly, but she was as slippery as a bar of soap. Her face was glowing red. Tears made puddles in her ears. She refused to open her eyes. She seemed to be doing anything she could to keep me out. She didn't want to listen, or be held, or even look at me. She was a turtle in her shell.

April was sitting on the bed and flipping pages in *The Baby Book*. "Here it is," April said. "It's called a breastfeeding strike." She read the description:

> Some babies abruptly refuse to breastfeed for several days, then with coaxing resume their previous breastfeeding routine. Humorously called a breastfeeding strike...

April stopped reading and looked at me. We were both thinking the same thing. Neither of us found this very humorous. April continued:

> ...this behavior is usually caused by physical upsets, such as teething, illness, or hospitalization, and emotional upsets, such as a recent move, illness in the mother, family discord, or the busy-ness syndrome (too many visitors, too many outside responsibilities, holiday stress, and so on).

April set the book on her lap and looked at me. Again we were thinking the same thing.

"That checklist sounds a lot like our last two weeks," April said.

I smiled.

Just for fun—since this was supposed to be humorous after all—we went back through the list and checked off six out of the seven possible causes for a breastfeeding strike, minus hospitalization—but you never knew, there was still tomorrow.

Teething. Check.

Illness. Check. (April and Alleke got my cold.)

Recent move. Check. (I was sitting on a pile of boxes while I wrote this.)

Illness in the mother. Check. (Again, April's cold)

Family discord. Check. (Moving was stressful.)

Busy-ness syndrome. Check. (We spent the weekend at a retreat in the mountains. Lots of new people, new job responsibilities, holiday stress, and one more place to temporarily call "home.")

I don't know why we needed a book to tell us our life was in chaos, but we did. The book told us that it was not normal to move to another country or to live in an apartment with a pile of boxes sitting in the middle of the floor.

Maybe Alleke was on strike.

I looked at her. She was whimpering, nearly asleep now from all her crying.

"Why don't you try to feed her again?" I asked.

April frowned. She had already tried three times.

She settled herself into bed and reached for Alleke. She pulled Alleke up close, and Alleke began to eat.

I listened as April sang Alleke a lullaby.

It was still early in the evening, but Alleke fell asleep and didn't wake up until the next morning. She may not have been on a breastfeeding strike, but she may have been striking for something else—a little rest and some time with Mom and Dad.

I got ready for bed, turned off the light, and got into bed.

Maybe I would go on strike too.

5 MONTHS, 26 DAYS
Loophole

Today I found my first good reason to let Alleke sit in front of the TV and watch movies all day.

April, Alleke and I were sitting at the table eating breakfast in silence. It was nearly eleven o'clock in the morning, but all three of us were still in our pajamas and looked like three junior high girls recovering from a sleepover.

Alleke was sick. She had spent most of the night crying and trying to get comfortable. Her forehead was warm to the touch like a radiator, and her blonde hair was wet and matted down.

I bit into my bagel, and as I thought about how to help Alleke feel better, and by extension, get a better night of sleep myself that night, I realized that one of the problems is that babies don't rest when they're sick. They keep going, doing whatever they normally do, and they don't stop.

Alleke, for example, kept trying to do her morning push-ups, but she was so tired, she just lay there like a dead fish. At lunch when she was in her high chair, she rested her head on the table while she ate her Cheerios.

If Alleke was going to get better soon, we had to find a way to get her to do nothing, to sit on her butt and be a couch potato. I ate more of my bagel and thought about this. The only time I had actually seen her do nothing was sometimes in the evenings when April and I would watch movies. Alleke would sit in front of the TV and stare.

So, after breakfast I made some calls, and within a few minutes had collected some Disney movies from the neighbors. Alleke watched closely as I bent down and pushed *Finding Nemo* into the DVD player, and the television screen came to life.

Alleke reached for April to pick her up. April looked at me and nodded towards Alleke's blankie lying on the floor, so I handed it to April as she picked up Alleke and sat down again on the couch. Alleke snuggled in and quietly watched as the little orange fish swam across the screen.

Today, television had saved the day.

5 MONTHS, 28 DAYS
Alleke's Worst Day

Alleke is sick

Alleke lay on the changing table while I sang her a song and fastened the Velcro straps on her diaper. It was early to be putting her to sleep, but she was nodding off already, fighting to keep her eyes open long enough to moan and reach for me to pick her up.

Alleke still had a cold and had spent most of the afternoon

resting her head on her mom's lap. She had rings around her eyes like red bruises, and when we put her down to play, she just sat there in the middle of her toys staring at nothing in particular.

As I lifted her from the changing table into my arms, she began to cry. She coughed, her lungs rattling, and dropped her head over my shoulder in defeat.

I walked into the bedroom and reached for the switch to turn on the light, but decided not to. This little girl was too tired for a bedtime story tonight.

Alleke chokes

I was on the couch in the living room when I heard a knock on our bedroom door. April was in the bedroom helping Alleke get to sleep, and this was our signal for telling each other when we needed something.

I cracked open the door and walked into the dark room. I could hear April singing a lullaby in the far corner, so I carefully felt my way across the room.

"Can you get the paracetamol?" April whispered into my ear while she rocked Alleke in her arms. "She has a fever," April added.

I traced my steps back to the door and left quietly. When I returned with the small bottle and syringe in my hand, the lamp was on in the room, and April and Alleke were sitting on the edge of the bed. Alleke's eyes were closed. She was mostly asleep, but she kept trying to climb up April's chest to get comfortable.

I pulled the liquid from the bottle into the syringe. April held Alleke's arms while I squeezed the medicine into her mouth. Alleke pulled away, squinted into the light, and began to cry.

The red liquid oozed out of the corners of her mouth. April frowned, then kissed Alleke on the forehead and said, "It's okay sweetie." April tipped Alleke's head back, and Alleke began to cry even harder as she squirmed around, pulled hard at April's arms, and tried to break free.

All of us wanted to get this over with, so I put the syringe into Alleke's mouth again and squeezed. Alleke's crying turned to gurgling, then suddenly stopped. Her eyes went wide, and she began gasping for air. She was choking on the medicine.

April sat her up and began banging on her back. Alleke still wasn't making a sound. She was frantic to breathe.

Something broke loose, and she heaved, water and everything else pouring into her lap. She breathed deep and began shrieking uncontrollably, refusing to be comforted. Her face was red with rage. She stopped to vomit again and collapsed against April's chest, whimpering.

Alleke falls off the bed

I was again on the couch in the living room, this time with April sitting next to me, when I heard a thump. It sounded like someone in another room had slammed a door. April looked at me, then jumped off the couch.

"Oh no," she said, "I left Alleke on our bed."

Alleke began screaming from the bedroom, and when April flung open the bedroom door, Alleke's crying echoed through the apartment like a police siren.

I followed April into the bedroom where she was holding Alleke in her arms. Alleke was thrashing around like a fish caught on a line and trying to push April away with her palms. She was crying with words, ones we still don't understand, as if she were asking us why all this was happening to her, especially all in one night.

This morning I woke up to Alleke practicing her words in bed. She sat between me and her mom repeating the same words like a mantra until she got them right, then moved on to new ones. She was very serious about the whole business, very dedicated, especially to be up practicing at such an early hour. But when I turned over to look at her, she stopped long enough to giggle at me (and my bed head) and reach over to push the end of my nose with her pointer finger.

I helped her slide off the bed, and she scooted off into the living room to look for toys while I lay there for a few moments before dragging myself out of bed, slipping on a pair of jeans, and following her out into the unknowns of a new day.

5 MONTHS, 31 DAYS
Funny Farm

Yesterday I walked into the living room, and April was cleaning and singing, "They're coming to take me away, ho ho, hee hee, ha ha, to the funny farm."

April caught me smiling, then realized she was singing.

"Maybe we should put on some music," she said, smiling too. She walked over and picked up the iPod off the stereo. "I'm in the mood for some Afro-Cuban All Stars. How about you, Alleke?"

April looked over at Alleke who was busy playing on the floor with a tractor.

The music started, and the room surged with Latin rhythms, first the keys walking back and forth, playfully, from one end of the scale to the other, followed by the steady grind of the percussion, and finally the old Cuban men singing their love songs.

April set the iPod down and began dancing, which I've come to believe is an involuntary reaction when it comes to music with this much groove. So I joined her, and we both danced, and we were very silly, since that's the only kind of dancing we know how to do. We laughed and twirled and pretended to tango.

That's when Alleke noticed us, finally. She took one look, fattened her lip, and began to cry. She flapped her arms, not sure where to go for comfort since both mom and dad were the ones terrorizing her this time.

April walked over and picked up Alleke, and we smiled at each other behind her back. We weren't sure what to think. Perhaps Alleke was upset for one of the following reasons:

a) our dancing was so bad we made a baby cry
b) we need to have more fun in our house
c) all of the above

I'm going with c.

6 MONTHS, 2 DAYS
Spilled Milk

I cut off a piece of banana and set it on the table in front of Alleke. April and I watched with the same curiosity as someone who had thrown peanuts to a monkey at the zoo as Alleke carefully picked up her first banana and held it in her hand like a prize. She licked it and then, as if returning to her most primal instinct, squished the banana in her fist. Banana pushed through the cracks in her fingers like Play-Doh. Some of it fell on the table in front of her, and some ran down her arm. Alleke giggled, dropped the rest of the banana on the floor, and clapped her hands.

I smiled and shook my head. Somehow I got the feeling I would be picking up food off the floor for the next decade until the motion had become an involuntary act—like digesting food.

I left the puddle of banana on the table in front of Alleke. She had to eat something, after all. So I cleaned her arms off with her bib, stuck her little fist in my mouth and sucked off the banana—which by the way, she thought was entirely hilarious— and bent over to pick up the banana off the floor.

Alleke must have been trying to see what I was doing because she bent over and peered through the narrow gap between the chair and the table. She squirmed in her chair, trying to see better, and that's when I noticed she was about to plant her forehead in the banana mush on the table.

Without thinking, I reached for her. My hand never got to her, though. I did stop her from sticking her forehead in the pile of banana, but not in a way either of us expected. Because what I didn't realize was that between Alleke and me was a glass of milk, a tall, full glass of milk, and when my hand came at her like a boxing glove, it knocked over that glass of milk so fast neither of us even knew what had happened.

I'd never thrown a glass of milk in someone's face before. It was my first time. I wasn't sure what would happen. I looked at Alleke, and she looked at me. She was covered in milk from the top of her head to the bottom of her bib. She looked like a little glazed donut. Milk was dripping off the ends of her eyelashes.

Alleke looked around and began to cry. She tried to wipe the milk out of her eyes with her fists and looked to her mom for help. It was April's turn to shake her head, and this time the gesture was meant for me. She got up, disappeared in the bathroom and returned with a bath towel in her hands. She looked at Alleke again, sized her up, and started to laugh.

Alleke looked serious for a moment, thinking, then must have decided it was okay to giggle too. She licked the milk from the corners of her mouth and belly laughed.

I chuckled too as I watched the milk drip off the end of the table and pool in the cracks in the hardwood floor.

Hmmm…what's that they say again about spilled milk?

6 MONTHS, 15 DAYS

Sweet Potato

"What's she doing?" I asked.

Alleke was sitting in her high chair, which was fastened to the end of the table. She was bent over the metal pole that runs the length of the high chair and holding onto it with both hands.

"I think she's trying to bite the pole," April said, looking closer.

Alleke sat there, completely still, which doesn't happen that often, and I could hear her teeth grinding like a mortal and pestle.

I grimaced. "That can't be good," I said.

"Alleke, honey," April said, trying to get her to stop.

Alleke looked up, noticed we were both watching her, then went back to work with the same concentration as someone eating corn on the sob.

I noticed the sweet potato sitting on the table in front of Alleke. It looked like a lump of red clay. I wondered why Alleke thought it was a good idea to try to eat a metal pole instead of a sweet potato. I remembered the tangy, bitter taste of rust and metal in my mouth. I swallowed hard.

"I have an idea," I said.

I took a glob of sweet potato between my fingers, and when Alleke looked up to see what I was doing, I smeared the sweet potato all over the pole, like I was frosting a cake.

"There," I said and smiled at Alleke.

April rolled her eyes.

Alleke hesitated, then touched the gooey pole with her finger. She looked at me, concerned.

Alleke had been outsmarted, which, believe it or not, doesn't happen that often. She accepted this, and so, decided to carry on. She bent over and bit into the pole like it was a candy bar.

April and I watched as Alleke slowly, but dutifully ate the potato off the pole, taking breaks between bites to chew and swallow, until the pole was nearly clean.

Feeling lucky, I spread more potato on the pole. She ate that too.

Alleke had eaten almost the whole slice of potato, which was more than she had ever eaten before.

7 MONTHS, 9 DAYS

Homecoming

I walked through the sliding door into the arrivals hall. I was almost home. I looked for the sign to the metro, then set down my bag and rummaged through it looking for my ticket.

Out of the corner of my eye I could see someone walking my way, so I looked up.

"Surprise," April said, "Alleke and I decided to come and meet you at the airport."

I left my bag on the ground, stood up, and embraced both of them. Alleke smiled with one finger in her mouth.

"Can I hold her?" I asked, not waiting for an answer.

I kissed Alleke on the nose, held her tight against my chest, and ran my fingers over her fuzzball head. I was bursting at the seams. I had missed my daughter.

I had been in Amsterdam at a conference for the last week, and the entire time I was gone I was wondering how Alleke would respond when I got home. This trip was the first time we had been apart since she was born seven months ago.

I held Alleke out so I could get a look at her. She was still smiling. Our eyes locked, and she recognized me. I'm not sure if she hadn't recognized me before, but at that moment, she recognized me as her dad.

Her emotions swept over her like a tsunami wave. Her mouth capsized. Tears flooded her eyes. She sobbed and gasped for breath like she was drowning. She must have realized just then that I had been gone and how that made her feel. She had missed me and hated it. Her emotions were too much all at once.

I handed Alleke back to April. Alleke burrowed her head into April's shoulder, and April rubbed her back and sang her a favorite song.

April and I talked a little, waiting, until eventually Alleke lifted her head and looked around. She saw me again, smiled, then buried her head back into April's shoulder. It was like she was looking at the sun. She could only look at me so long before her emotions rushed over her and she had to hide, safe, in mom's chest. We played this game for minutes until finally she giggled and reached for my nose.

I took her, of course, and tossed her in the air. She laughed. April picked up my backpack, put it on, and we headed for home.

7 MONTHS, 24 DAYS
Urban Jungle

I got this email from my mom-in-law this afternoon:

Spain (Country threat level - 3): Violent clashes occurred in Madrid early this morning. Hundreds of people erected barricades with burning debris, set trashcans on fire and knocked down telephone booths. The protesters also attacked police officers with rocks and other objects, while officers used rubber bullets and tear gas to control the crowd. At least 65 people — including 21 police officers — were injured in the clashes, while eight others were arrested.

I opened a new email and wrote a reply:

Hi Mom,

Yeah, actually, this happened around the corner from our apartment. As for our involvement, I remember waking up at 2 am and hearing people cheering in the streets. This morning we got up and went outside. Only the street cleaners were there.

Kelly

I guess that explains why yesterday when I took Alleke for a walk the main square in our neighborhood was empty except for clusters of police officers wearing bulletproof vests and standing at all the entrances.

That was odd, but I didn't think much of it at the time because that's our neighborhood. It's a hodgepodge, a zoo of humans, a container for people who don't fit anywhere else. Our neighborhood is a place where people dabble and experiment. Self expression is written in spray paint all over the doors and walls of our buildings. People come to our neighborhood to make mistakes.

I wondered about this neighborhood when we emerged from the metro into the daylight the day we came to look at our apartment for the first time. I saw the statue in the square where instead of lifting a sword, the hero had an empty beer bottle stuck in his fist. I saw the girls waiting in their short skirts hollering after potential customers, and the man slumped against the doorway trying to hold the needle still against his arm.

I also saw trees. I hadn't seen them before, growing straight up out of the concrete. I saw old people, the men chatting on benches in the square, the women pulling carts of fresh groceries back to their apartments to make lunch, and kids—kids everywhere. Some wearing school uniforms and buying baguettes for their mothers. The smaller ones climbing through the jungle gym. And the babies being pushed around in strollers all over the place, so everyone could enjoy them.

I feel stupid sometimes, and stubborn, for wanting and choosing to live smack dab in the middle of the city. I feel like April and I always choose to do things the hard way. We try something new instead of sticking to what we know. We make our parents squirm.

I don't actually know why we live in this neighborhood—why I felt so strongly about it. Maybe because I want Alleke to grow up knowing that even in places like our neighborhood, the ones where every once in a while people get drunk and start smashing telephone booths and setting trash cans on fire, even here we can find beauty...and God...if we look for them.

Our friends Byron and Lisa live in Portugal with their three teenage boys and a little girl and happen to be the best parents I know. I was talking with Lisa recently about our move into the city and how April and I felt like we didn't know what we were getting ourselves into. We were both from small towns in Iowa. I wondered if we could be good parents in the city since we knew so little about urban life.

I don't remember exactly what Lisa said, but it was something like this: The question in many ways is not where is the best place for Alleke to live, but where is the best place for me, for us, as her parents to live because wherever we are living our lives fully is where and how she is going to learn to live her life fully as well.

I don't know if living in the city makes sense for us. We'll have to learn how to survive in this urban jungle. But maybe what's most important is that I feel like I can be myself here.

Adriana

I apologized to Adriana at the front door, even before I introduced her to April, and even before I actually had anything to apologize about. We are new parents after all, and Adriana was our first babysitter that wasn't a family member or close friend.

Although Adriana has spent the last ten years nannying children, which means she has almost ten years more experience than I do, I just knew April and I were going to spend the next two hours explaining all kinds of unnecessary details to Adriana about how to sanitize Alleke's bottles (the ones she doesn't even use anymore), the exact position we use when we put her to sleep (which, I should have guessed, changed later this week because everything changes every week), and Alleke's bedtime routine from beginning to end, including the book we read and the song we sing (at which point Adriana, who is from Colombia, smiled and said she would bring her own book, in Spanish).

We went completely over the top. I'm sure Adriana left thinking we need more counseling. I bet the moment she stepped out our front door into the street, she felt like someone had let her off a leash. Still, if I had the chance to do the night over again, I would do it exactly the same way. Asking a stranger to take care of your child is not easy.

I'm not so concerned about finding a babysitter that cares for Alleke exactly the same way I do. I'm not looking for a robot. I'm looking for someone who not only cares for Alleke, but also cares about her. Adriana obviously loves kids. She kept Alleke on her lap the whole evening. And in spite of the fact that we are the first parents she's met that use cloth diapers and sleeps with Alleke in our bed and wear our baby on our back, Adriana didn't let our crazy side stop her from getting to know Alleke and even having a little fun with her. At one point Adriana picked up the baby carrier and tried to put it on. She got so tangled up with the straps that her hands were literally tied behind her back. She started giggling and before long we were all laughing, even Alleke.

I want Alleke to know from her own experience that she can be cared for by people who are very different from her mom and dad—people that read bedtime stories in a different language or sing her to sleep with a lullaby she's never heard before or who don't have the same blonde hair as she and her parents do. I hope Alleke learns that the way we do things doesn't matter as much as why we do them.

8 MONTHS, 27 DAYS
Vienna

The woman at the far side of the room got up and walked over to see what I was doing. My chair was pushed back, and I was leaning over a restaurant table trying to figure out how to attach Alleke's portable high chair.

The woman bent over and looked under the table. "I don't think that's going to work," she said. "Why don't you have my table?" She pointed to where she had been sitting at a small table with a red and white checkered tablecloth, a glass of wine, and an open newspaper.

"Thank you," April said.

The woman smiled, and we followed her to her table. She

said a few words in German to the customers sitting at the next table, then moved her things to their table. "I think this is better for you," she said. She smiled again and took a seat at the next table.

I fastened the high chair to the end of the table, put Alleke in it, and sat down to look at the menu. I was relieved to discover that although all the menu items were listed in German, underneath they were also translated into English in italics. We were visiting Vienna for the first time to attend a conference for work and had wandered into the busy café across the street from our hostel to look for food. I flipped through the laminated pages and decided on a stew with dumplings.

Alleke sat next to me, kicking her legs, shaking her rattle, and flirting with the waitresses walking to and from the kitchen.

"Did you look at the walls?" April said while she stared at the wall behind Alleke.

"No," I said, noticing them for the first time. They were covered with bumper stickers and posters and hand-written letters and kids' drawings and newspaper clippings and decorated certificates and family photos.

The room was cluttered with paper, especially our corner. I don't know how I missed this at first. Some pieces covered up others, as if the walls were an ongoing project, still being added to, new memories covering over older ones.

"She must be the owner," April said and pointed to one of the pictures. "She's in most of these."

I looked more closely at the picture of a young woman with her hand on the head of a child and her head resting on the shoulder of a young man. She clearly resembled the woman whose newspaper and glass of wine were sitting at the table next to us. I looked at other pictures, and there she was with her gray hair.

I've never actually seen a clearer picture of a person's life than on the walls of that restaurant. The woman's name was Inga. She had been married with children and traveled a lot. Her husband had died years back, and her children had grown up and moved away. She was still here, putting her life into this place, the family restaurant.

"This is for the baby," I heard someone say over my shoulder.

I looked away from the pictures on the wall. It was Inga. She set a small plate of food down on the table between Alleke and me. I smiled awkwardly, embarrassed at first, as if I had just been caught looking through someone's kitchen cupboards, but she just glanced at the wall, smiled, and patted Alleke on the head.

"I think you'll like this," she said to Alleke and winked at her.

I looked at the food on the plate. I had no idea what it was. It looked like a pancake, cut up into bite-sized pieces, sprinkled with powdered sugar and drizzled with chocolate.

I wouldn't think of feeding something like this to Alleke, not something with sugar and chocolate, but I picked up the fork, and I fed it to her anyway. I leaned over and whispered in Alleke's ear, "Eat up little girl because you're getting away with murder today."

I can't think of many situations where I would value something more than doing what's best for my child, but that day I decided to feed my daughter junk food. Part of it, I suppose, is I didn't dare to say no, but I think most of it had to do with an appreciation for Inga and all the other people like her in our life. I thought of the people at our bakery who sneak Alleke suckers when we're not looking, or the man who always stops us to talk in front of his fish shop. Today we were celebrating these people who don't have to care about us, but do anyway, simply because they want to.

First Steps

Yesterday Alleke played with power tools. She sat perched on my dad's knee and watched carefully as he helped her squeeze the trigger on the drill, the motor whining as the screws turned into the end of the wood plank sitting on the living room floor. They were building a shelf for our DVDs.

My parents are visiting for two weeks, and my dad brought his drill with him from the United States. I had asked him on the phone a few weeks earlier if he would, and he said yes. With the same excitement as when I asked him to be the best man at my wedding, he began thinking out loud about how he would make room for the drill in his suitcase.

My dad was used to bringing his drill along with him whenever he visited family. For years he had been bringing his drill to my brother and sister's houses, not to mention my grandma's house. He built my grandma's house with his own bare hands (and the drill, of course). He had helped my brother finish off the basement in his new house a few years back, and he's still rewiring my sister's basement after it flooded in May from a broken water pipe.

But this was the first time he was bringing his drill to my house. I guess it had never crossed my mind before to ask, or for that matter, I guess I had never had a list of things for him to do around house before either.

Things had changed. I had a baby now. I was a dad, and my parents were now Grandpa and Grandma. Grandpa had his drill in his suitcase because our relationship was different now. I just didn't know how.

Grandpa and Grandma arrived, and although I had to work some, we talked about doing something fun on Wednesday morning. I was used to having fun with my parents when they visited. We loved to travel together. We had sipped Moroccan mint tea at a teahouse in Granada and marveled at the snowflake ceilings of the Alhambra. We had lost track of time on the beach in San Sebastian. We had raised a glass of sangria to the flamenco dancers at La Carbonería in Seville. We had eaten paella in Valencia.

Most of these things sounded tiring now that Alleke was in the picture, and since she would be coming along with us on Wednesday morning, I decided to keep our plans simple. We would stop at our favorite bakery down the street for coffee, then walk over to see the temporary Van Gogh exhibit at the Thyssen Museum. That was the plan.

Alleke woke up a little later than usual, so Grandpa got out his drill and began working on the shelf we wanted in the kitchen for the microwave. I sat down on the couch and wrote some work emails. By the time Alleke was up and playing on the floor in the living room, Grandpa was drilling anchor holes in the wall, and Grandma was doing a load of laundry. We decided to wait to leave until our projects were finished, but when they were, Alleke was in bed again for her morning nap. Again, she slept later than usual. In fact, she normally sleeps an hour in the mornings, and she slept two and a half hours. When she woke up, Grandma and I were already busy in the kitchen making lunch. Grandpa was fixing two squeaky fans, and the parts were lying all over the floor in the living room.

The morning had come and gone, and we were still at home. We had not had an adventure. We had gotten some work done around the house.

Later that night when Alleke and Grandpa and Grandma were in bed, and April and I were left sitting on the couch in the living room talking, I told April I thought our lives were boring now. Being adventurous was too much work. I wanted to stay home for the rest of my life.

I was right, of course, about our lives being boring—at least if what I meant by "boring" was staying at home. We didn't leave the apartment much the rest of the week. Grandpa finished all the fix-it projects on our list, and then some, and I wrote lots of emails, and Grandma washed more clothes.

But, we also cooked and ate meals together, and we sat on the couches and read books, and we watched TV, and we spent lots of time on the floor with Alleke holding her hands and coaching her because Grandpa said he wanted to see his granddaughter take her first steps before he left.

And you'll never guess what happened Saturday afternoon. Grandpa and Grandma were sitting on the living room floor, and Alleke was standing next to the footstool, and I was writing emails, and Alleke let go of the footstool and took two steps. Grandpa and Grandma got all excited, and April came running from the kitchen, and we danced around the room like we were living the happy ending of a fairy tale.

I'm still waiting for our next adventure with Grandpa and Grandma, and I'm hoping it includes tulip fields, lots of people on bicycles, a windmill or two, and a few more Van Gogh paintings, but for now, I've come to the place where I'm willing to say normal life is worth living, even when grandparents are visiting. A vacation at home may be boring, but that's where real life happens. I guess this time I was ready for Grandpa and Grandma to see that too.

9 MONTHS, 16 DAYS
Play

Last night Alleke and I were sitting on a park bench in the square near our house. Alleke was sitting on my lap, and we were watching the dogs—chasing after tennis balls, lapping water out of the fountain, and running circles around their owners, looking for attention.

I got thinking about last year at this time and realized I am less busy now than I was then. I would have thought being the dad of a ten-month-old, I would be busier, but I've found that I actually have more time for things like sitting on park benches.

The difference is my life is scheduled now. The hard part is I almost never get to do what I want to do when I want to do it, unless it's in the schedule, which means I've learned to measure time by naps and meals and dirty diapers and bedtime stories. But, Alleke's schedule includes something mine almost never did. Play time.

Alleke gives me permission to play every day. She likes sitting on park benches and watching the dogs digging in the dirt, so I get to come along.

It's great to be a dad.

10 MONTHS, 6 DAYS
Sandbox

"I think she has something in her mouth," I said as I glanced over my shoulder at Rubén's mom. Rubén, another little boy we had met at the playground, was sitting in the sand next to Alleke playing with a plastic rake.

I leaned in for a closer look.

Alleke's lips were pressed together in a fish face, and her jaw was going up and down like she was chewing on twenty pieces of bubble gum all at once.

"Here, let me see," I said, playing dentist. I stuck my finger in her mouth.

Alleke shook her head and turned away.

I reached again, and this time she surrendered, lifting her head and sticking out her tongue.

"Oh, that's bad," I heard Rubén's mom say from behind me.

There on Alleke's tongue, as if being presented to me on a miniature platter, was a short, soggy cigarette butt.

10 MONTHS, 28 DAYS
Personal Choice

Alleke waddled over and sat down in front of the front door. April and I watched from the couches. It was six o'clock in the afternoon according to the clock sitting on the bookshelf, and we were still in our pajamas. It was our day off, and we had no intention of leaving the house.

Alleke turned around to look at us and began to cry. Or at least she tried very hard to cry. She meant to cry for real, but only managed to whine a little, which sounded like a sparrow with hiccups (or at least how I would imagine a sparrow with hiccups would sound, that is, if they get hiccups, which I'm not sure about).

April and I giggled, which Alleke didn't like very much. I think she was disappointed in us and frustrated that we didn't seem to understand what she wanted, so, in an effort to clarify her intentions, she began pounding on the door with the palm of her hand. She stopped to look at us again, like we were playing a game of charades, and she was waiting for us to guess the easy answer.

"I think she wants to get out of the house and do something," April said. "I think she's bored." April looked at me.

"I think you're right," I said.

Now that Alleke could pull herself to her feet and stagger around the house like Frankenstein, she could also communicate more. She had more choices to make, which meant she could be more of her own person. She could decide whether she wanted to play by herself with her blocks in the living room or help mom pot plants in the kitchen or get dad's attention at his desk by pulling DVDs off the shelf.

And now Alleke could also communicate whether she was bored with being at home. Suddenly, just like that, it mattered what she thought. From now on April and I had to figure into our plans not just what Alleke needed, but also what she wanted.

I rubbed my eyes, then stretched, reaching for the ceiling.

"I guess we could go to the park for a while," I said to April. "I mean if that's what Alleke wants."

11 MONTHS, 16 DAYS
Pointing

Alleke scratched at my neck until she found my shirt collar. Using it as a handle, she yanked down and pulled herself up high enough to sling her arm over my shoulder and point into the darkness.

I turned around and squinted into the dim corner of the room. I didn't see anything unusual, just our bed. Alleke began to cry.

Alleke had recently learned to point at things, and while this had seemed helpful at first, in the end it just meant she had to have anything she could point at. If Alleke could point at the iPod hanging around the neck of the man standing next to us on the bus, Alleke had to have that iPod, now. She had earned it with her pointing.

Unfortunately for Alleke life doesn't work that way, and for the moment, it was time to sleep, not to point. I pried her fingers from my collar and cradled her in my arms again, humming a lullaby.

Alleke lay there, but only long enough to figure out what she was going to do next. She played dead, slumping over like a bag of potatoes, her weight loose in my arms. While I scrambled to get a hold of her, she reached around me and pointed at the corner of the room again.

I got a hold of her, eventually, and while she was still pointing, I decided to carry her across the room and dump her on the bed.

"Now what?" I said and glared at her with my hands on my hips.

She looked around, perhaps realizing that now that she was here, there wasn't much to see, like a trip to Wall Drug after passing all those billboards. In the end, Alleke decided to cut her losses and move on. She looked at me and pointed at the bedroom door. She wanted to go into the living room.

I didn't feel like playing Alleke's pointing game, but I didn't feel like putting her to sleep anymore either. I was tired, probably more tired than she was, which I can only guess is why I decided it was actually a good idea to go into the living room. After all, it was a win-win situation, I told myself. Alleke could have her way, and I could have mine. We still had *Finding Nemo* in the house, which meant I could put on the movie, sit in the rocking chair with Alleke and close my eyes, and let the movie put Alleke to sleep. My work was done.

Alleke watched from my arms as I put in the DVD. We settled into the chair, and I closed my eyes. Alleke held her blankie close, laid her head on my chest, and watched the movie.

While Alleke was happy to watch for a while, soon she was sitting up and looking around. She began pointing over my shoulder in the direction of the kitchen, and when I ignored her and pretended to be asleep, she squawked and twisted my nose.

I sat up and glared at her again, then without saying anything, got up and walked into the kitchen, the whole time Alleke pointing me in the right direction.

In the kitchen, Alleke stopped pointing and started looking around like she was trying to find something. I looked around too. I saw Alleke's sippy cup sitting on the counter, and although she had just eaten dinner and had had a drink before she went to bed, maybe she wanted some milk before she went to sleep, I thought.

I pulled open the door to the freezer and dug around until I found a plastic bottle of milk. Alleke recognized the bottle immediately, grabbed it from my hand, and began sucking on the lid.

"You want some milk?" I asked, laughing at the understatement.

Alleke continued to suck on the lid while I warmed up some water on the stove, and when I finally handed her the sippy cup with milk, she gulped it down, only gasping for air when necessary, like a basketball player in the huddle in the last minutes of a tied game.

Minutes later Alleke was sound asleep in her own bed, and I was cleaning up toys in the living room, piecing together the events of the evening to make sense of them.

Alleke had wanted milk from the beginning and had tried to communicate that to me the best she could, first pointing at the bed where mom often fed her at night, then to the living room where mom usually was if dad was putting her to sleep. When she realized mom wasn't home, she pointed to the kitchen where she got milk in a cup sometimes.

I laughed because we hadn't fed her milk from a cup in over two months. Somehow she had remembered where to find it.

11 MONTHS, 23 DAYS
Yes and No

Alleke toddled over to the shelf of DVDs next to the TV. She stood on her tippy toes and reached, just able to pull one off the shelf. The DVD tumbled to the floor. She picked it up with both hands and looked it over like she was dumpster diving and had found her treasure. She turned the DVD over and looked at the back, then stuck it in her mouth to see how it tasted.

I watched from my desk in the corner of the room and smiled, astonished that my daughter was in the DVDs again, even though I had told her "No" three times in the last half hour, and not to mention she must have stepped over five or six of her favorite toys to get to the DVD shelf.

Alleke's back was to me, so when I said her name, "Alleke," even gently, she startled. Then she froze. She tossed the DVD and bolted for the kitchen, and since she's still not steady on her legs, she looked like a wobbly circus performer on stilts fleeing the scene of the crime.

I got up out of my chair, walked into the kitchen, and picked her up. We walked back into the living room and sat on the couch. We sat there, and I played with Alleke's fuzzy blonde hair and thought about my friend Gwyneth who is a trained Montessori instructor.

Gwyneth said to me once that it's important to create an environment in our home where our child is allowed to play with anything she can reach. Gwyneth didn't tell me why this was important, but I suppose it's because the job of a child is to explore her world, but a young child isn't old enough to understand why she can play with one thing, but not another. As Alleke's parents, we want to make doing her job as easy as possible, so we try to create an environment where she can play with anything she can reach.

April and I had removed most of the things around the house that we didn't want Alleke to play with (i.e. potted plants, sandals, which she had insisted on licking like a lollipop, my mountain bike, and the telephone), but there were still some forbidden items, and I found myself still saying, "No, Alleke" all the time.

I couldn't remember the last time I had said, "Yes, Alleke."

So, while we sat there on the couch, I began telling Alleke all the things she could do, and the ones that I liked to watch her do too.

"Yes, Alleke can give her dad kisses."

"Yes, Alleke can look at books."

"Yes, Alleke can stand or sit or crawl or walk."

"Yes, Alleke can stack blocks."

"Yes, Alleke can even climb steps."

The list went on, obvious at times ("Yes, Alleke has blue eyes") and hopeful ("Yes, Alleke can listen to the Afro-Cuban All Stars with her dad, anytime she wants") and on to the absurd ("Yes, Alleke can play in one of those pools full of plastic balls that they have at amusement parks because I loved those as a kid and I would never deny you that") and sometimes diplomatic ("Yes, Alleke can go to the park later if her dad can get some work done first").

I probably said the word "yes" a hundred times.

I know that outside of our little apartment there are many things that Alleke can't do. Licking those greasy poles on the metro comes to mind. Alleke is always reaching for them. She also can't eat leaves in the park or play with wine glasses at restaurants or pull books off the shelf at the library. When we leave the house, I say one "no" after another.

Alleke turns one next Wednesday, and like a teenager getting keys to her first car, I'm sure Alleke will become even more independent in the coming year as walking—and running away from her parents—become second-nature to her. That's why I'd like to think of our home as a place where we say "yes" for as long as possible. I don't have much control over what happens beyond our front door, but here at home things are different, and hopefully this place pulls our "yes" and our "no" into balance. Hopefully, here, Alleke feels free to explore her world.

PART III

Toddler

Independence Day

I'm beginning to think of last Wednesday less as Alleke's first birthday and more as her Independence Day.

Last night April and I sat on the couches and talked after Alleke was in bed. At one point April looked at me, puzzled, and said, "I barely saw Alleke tonight. Did you have her?"

"Not exactly," I said.

Troy had also celebrated his birthday recently, so we had thrown him a surprise party at his house. I had been working for a few days straight, however, and I hadn't seen much of Alleke. So, even though we were at a party, I decided to spend some time with my daughter.

Alleke had already run off somewhere, so I began looking around for her until I found her in her friend Nic's bedroom digging through toys. When I came in, she glanced up at me and handed me a yellow, wooden block, as if to say, "Take this. You'll need it."

She toddled to the door, looked back over her shoulder to make sure I was following, and disappeared into the hallway. I followed.

First we found Meaghan, who was standing at the end of the hallway with a camera. It was her dad's birthday, and her mom said she could take pictures. So, she lined up Alleke (giggling) and her friend Laura against the wall and took glamour shots.

Next we wandered into the living room and found Grandma and Papa, my in-laws, who had come to visit for Alleke's birthday. Papa sat on the couch with a bowl of popcorn, and Alleke stood next to him while he inspected each kernel, bit off the hard bits, and handed the kernels to Alleke to eat.

Later we found Nic sitting at the table with his friends playing a game he had made up using his transformer collection and a chessboard.

Anyway, I mention Meaghan, Papa and Nic simply to illustrate that Alleke and I spent the entire evening with Alleke's friends, wandering from room to room until we had found all of them. My role was simple—I had to carry the yellow, wooden block. Whenever Alleke found someone she wanted to play with, she would take the block from my hand and offer it to the person to see if he or she wanted to play. If not, she would hand the block back to me, and off we would go, looking for Alleke's next friend.

I suspect Alleke knew all along that she didn't need me to carry around that yellow, wooden block for her. I think she just didn't know what else to do with me. She wanted to spend time with her friends—it was a party after all—but she didn't want me to feel unwanted, so she gave me a job to do.

1 YEAR, 8 DAYS
Bad Influence

Papa and I sat on a park bench in the square and watched Alleke as she puttered around, stopping occasionally to study the fallen leaves.

A dad pushing his daughter in a stroller bought a balloon from the vender standing in the middle of the square and walked over. He took his daughter out of the stroller and set her down in front of Alleke. The two little girls stared at each other, as if wildly fascinated to finally find someone else just their size, then greeted each other in the customary way by petting each other's noses.

The dad crouched down with the pink balloon, which had been twisted up to look like a dog, and handed it to his daughter. He smiled at Alleke.

Alleke walked over and took the balloon from the little girl to get a better look at it. The little girl just smiled and clapped her hands.

I stood up from where I was sitting on the bench and walked over. I figured this was as good a time as any to teach Alleke how to share. I got down on my knees next to Alleke and explained the whole thing to her, careful to include gestures I thought she would understand. When I finished, I walked Alleke over to where the little girl was now playing in the leaves. I nodded at Alleke, pointed in the direction of the little girl, and waited.

Alleke looked down at the balloon she was holding and then looked up at me. She didn't seem to know what to do next. She just stood there. I glanced at the little girl's dad who was smiling politely, and I shrugged my shoulders.

Alleke watched carefully as I took the balloon from her hands and handed it back to the little girl. Immediately Alleke grabbed the balloon again and handed it to me, as if to say, "Here, I think you dropped this." She seemed pleased with herself for being helpful.

"No," I said and shook my head. I handed the balloon back to the little girl. We were going to get this right.

Alleke glared at me with that same look of injustice she gives me when she catches me trying to skip pages in her story books at night when I'm tired, as if the illusion that parents always know what's best had just been lifted and the very foundation of what is right and wrong had been chipped like a china cup. We had just disagreed about this balloon, and she was mad.

She began to cry. Regardless of what I wanted, she wanted that balloon, so she reached for it.

The dad smiled politely again. He reached down, took the balloon from his daughter, and untied a part of the balloon so it was in two parts. He handed one of the parts to his daughter and the other to Alleke.

Alleke screamed and pushed it away. She shook her head and pointed at the balloon the man had given to his daughter.

The man frowned.

"I'm sorry," I said.

He didn't say anything.

He handed me the balloon, lifted his daughter into her stroller, and pushed her away. I watched as he reached the far side of the square and stopped there. He lifted his daughter out of the stroller and sat down on a bench. He didn't have somewhere else to be. He just didn't want his daughter to play with mine. She was a bad influence.

1 YEAR, 13 DAYS
Oh Ye of Little Faith

So far in my thinking, I've discovered two basic parenting styles.

Parent as Expert

In the first parenting style, the parent is the expert. When the baby is born, her mind is like a blank slate without any rules for understanding the world around her. The parent, in contrast, knows the rules from experience and can train the child to behave appropriately.

Someone who uses this parenting style might train his child to take scheduled naps throughout the day because he knows naps are an appropriate behavior for a baby. The baby doesn't know this is an appropriate behavior, but the parent does, and feels it's his responsibility to train his child to take her naps.

Baby as Expert

In the second parenting style, the baby is the expert. When the baby is born, the parent focuses on learning how to listen to his baby's cues, trusting the baby will "tell" him when she needs something, like a nap or a diaper change or something to eat.

Someone using this parenting style might only put his baby down for a nap when he notices the normal signs that she's tired.

I have found this distinction between parenting styles helpful because when April and I disagree about how we parent Alleke, it usually comes down to our default parenting styles, which are different.

April and I have agreed to use the Baby as Expert parenting style, mostly because April is Alleke's primary caretaker at this point and it makes sense for us to use her default parenting style, which is Baby as Expert.

Also, I like this parenting style, even though it's not my default. It makes sense to me, and it fits our personalities. Our close friends tell us we listen well and like to encourage others, so we're building on our strengths by using this style.

Still, regardless of which parenting style I like the most, the Parent as Expert is my default, and it's the one I fall back on when I make decisions about parenting Alleke.

Recently April and I went for a walk to talk, and I told April I was nervous about Alleke being twelve months old and not eating solid foods. At six months we had started giving her solid foods at meals, and we hadn't forced her to eat anything. We just left the food there on the table in front of her, and we trusted she would begin eating it when she was ready.

Six months later, nothing had changed. During meals Alleke would play with her food like it was another toy, and she was content to breastfeed. If we were going to wait for Alleke to tell us when she wanted to stop breastfeeding and start eating solid foods, we were essentially waiting for a bus that was never going to arrive.

"We have to think ahead," I added, "and start teaching her now what we want her to do three months from now."

I expected April to disagree with me. I expected her to say something about being patient and about how Alleke would tell us when she was ready to move on, if we were willing to listen to her. But that's not what April said. She told me I was right, and she sighed. She told me she was willing to rethink our strategy.

A few days later we sat down for dinner, and while April and I ate our chili, Alleke nibbled on a block of cheddar cheese. The following evening we went with some friends to an Ecuadorian restaurant that's decorated like the hold of a pirate ship, and Alleke picked at some rice. Then she began eating the beans off April's plate, and after that, begged for pieces of plantain. Eventually we left her to chew on corn on the cob, so we could eat our own food.

Alleke hasn't stopped eating since then. She eats three meals a day plus snacks in between, and she's choosing to breastfeed less. (Not to mention her poop smells really bad now.)

I'd be a liar if I told you I had faith in Alleke that she would begin eating by herself when she was ready. Faith is believing in something you can't see with your own eyes. But I am a believer. I've seen it happen. We waited for Alleke to tell us when she was ready to eat, and she did it all by herself.

As Alleke becomes more independent, and begins to rely more on her thoughts and feelings and less on her instinct, she will expect us to set limits for her, to tell her what's right and wrong, and to be the Parent as Expert. Still, I hope I remember that she is an expert too, that I need to listen to her telling me what she needs, and that I can trust her to tell me when she's ready to grow.

1 YEAR, 29 DAYS

I'm Big. She's Small.

April watched from a bench close by as I lifted Alleke into my arms and set her again at the top of the slide. Alleke bit her lip with determination as she wiggled her way forward until her weight pulled her over the edge, and she slid to the bottom. All the while, I watched her head to make sure she wouldn't bump it at the bottom. She was convinced she could do the slide all by herself, but I wasn't—not yet.

At the bottom of the slide, she turned around and lowered herself into the sand, then darted off towards the entrance, a small break in the fence surrounding the playground.

April got up from the bench and walked over. By the time we reached the entrance to the playground, Alleke was half way across the square, standing along the sidelines of a volleyball game being played by teens who had strung up a net between two lampposts.

We walked over. By then Alleke had spotted the ramp that connects the lower and upper levels of the square. She was at the bottom testing her footing on the incline. It wasn't long before she was taking careful steps to the top.

"I'll get her," I said, glancing at April as I loosened my hand from hers and stepped away.

"Why?" April asked.

I stopped and turned.

"What do you mean?" I asked.

"I mean why do you have to get her?"

I looked at the ground, thinking. "I don't know," I said and shrugged my shoulders. "I guess I just don't want her to go over there."

"But why?" April asked again.

"I don't know," I said, holding out my hands. I grinned.

"That's not a good enough reason," April said. She looked over my shoulder at Alleke nearing the top of the ramp.

"Fine," I said, watching Alleke too.

April was right, of course. In fact, she often catches me telling Alleke not to do something for no good reason. She often asks me to explain the reason why I am telling Alleke not to do something, and often I don't have a reason.

I guess I'm surprised at how many times, without thinking, I put my wants and needs before Alleke's because I'm the parent and she's the daughter. I'm the adult, and she's the child. I'm big, and she's small.

1 YEAR, 1 MONTH, 29 DAYS

Erica

This morning I ran into Erica on the street. She was dressed in her normal clothes, not her uniform from the bread shop.

"I just got off work," she said, anticipating my first question. "I'm just running home to get a quick bite to eat."

She looked up the street.

"Do you live near here?"

"Just around the corner," I said. "How about you?"

"Two streets down."

I nodded.

"Oh, by the way," she said, as if remembering something important to tell me, "Your daughter is so beautiful." She said this like it was a new revelation, and not something she tells me from behind the cash register every time I go to buy bread.

We began to walk, and she grinned for a while, probably

thinking about our little girl in pigtails roaming around the bread shop offering her half-eaten croissant to the customers.

"I would love to take your daughter for a walk sometime," she said with a sigh, still daydreaming.

I smiled.

"Okay," I said.

She stopped and looked at me.

"Really?" she asked, concerned.

"Sure, you can take Alleke for a walk," I said. "She loves going for walks."

Erica looked at me a while longer, then shrugged her shoulders. "Okay," she said.

We decided on Sunday afternoon, and she took down my phone number.

"I'll give you a call," she said.

Then she thought for a moment.

"You should ask your wife about this."

I laughed and nodded.

"Okay, I'll ask my wife."

It wasn't until Sunday when we were standing in the street, and I lifted Alleke into Erica's arms, and Alleke turned and reached for me, that I realized Alleke didn't know this woman, and neither did I.

Erica was, as April had warned me, a stranger. She wasn't a babysitter. She wasn't a close friend. She was the woman who worked at the bread shop and played with Alleke when we came in to buy bread.

I stood there and watched as Erica carried my daughter down the street and turned the corner out of sight. I walked across the street to our friends' house where there was a Christmas party, and I sat on their couch and didn't say a word.

I had gone skiing in the Alps once with a group of fifteen, and by the afternoon I found myself alone with the only expert skier in the group. She skied most weekends, but avoided ski resorts altogether because they didn't challenge her anymore. She would find a mountain she didn't know, hike to the top with her skis on her back, and ski down in virgin snow.

She was bored, of course, skiing with me, and resisted until late afternoon to ask if I would be willing to hop over the snow fence and ski down the backside of the mountain, out of bounds, in virgin snow.

Once I managed to block out April's last words to me before I left, which were, "Have fun skiing, but don't do anything stupid," I said yes, because most importantly I wanted to be the kind of person that could say I had skied down the backside of a mountain in virgin snow in the Swiss Alps. What I didn't realize was I actually had to do it first.

I spent the afternoon falling down the mountain, and I learned that virgin snow is like one giant bubble bath where you can't see what's under all those bubbles, including rocks, even boulders, caverns, and drop-offs. It wasn't until we reached the bottom that she bothered to explain what to do in case of an avalanche.

It was dangerous, and I was unprepared, and while it might be impressive to mention at dinner parties that I have skied down the backside of a mountain in virgin snow in the Swiss Alps, I would be embarrassed to admit as much, and more importantly, I am convinced it was not worth the risk. It wasn't fun either.

When I told Erica she could take Alleke for a walk, I got ahead of myself. I was thinking about what would happen after everything went well and about how I would to be the kind of person who could say we had friends in the neighborhood and trusted them with our kids. I pictured my family walking into the bread shop where Erica works and everyone knowing our names. It would be like watching a rerun of *Friends*.

What I didn't realize was I actually had to leave Alleke with a stranger first before any of this could happen. I sat there on the couch, glaring at the clock, and thinking about all the things I didn't know about Erica, and all the things she might not know about herself, especially when it came to caring for children.

Erica called an hour later. She must have known I was sitting there on the couch because she said she was calling to let me know that Alleke was doing fine and hadn't cried yet. They were kicking a ball around in the square down the street, and they had taken some cute photos together that she would show me when I picked up Alleke.

I felt much better, like someone coming out of his house after a hurricane to find that the shutters were still on the windows. The howling winds of worry had quieted, and I was left with the simple realization that I was an irresponsible parent.

Alleke is her own person, but at her age, she depends on me to protect her and keep her safe. It's one thing for me to take my own risks, knowing there may be consequences, but hoping for the best. It's another thing to put Alleke at risk when she doesn't know better. She doesn't know strangers can be strange. She doesn't know what I know, which is that if something terrible happened to her, both of us would have to live with the consequences.

1 YEAR, 2 MONTHS
Park Bench

I sat on the park bench, my arm slung over the back of it, and watched my daughter balance herself—not very well, I might add—at the front edge.

She was contemplating whether to jump.

I was surprised she had even managed to step to the edge of the bench. As observed, there was indeed a very fine line between bravery and stupidity.

However, at that very moment I wondered less what Alleke would do, and more about what I was or was not going to do as her parent and protector. Was I the kind of parent who would back her away from the edge of the bench? Or, would I let her fall?

I watched as she teetered at the edge of the bench, then lost her balance and fell in the dirt. She cried, and I picked her up. I dusted her off, set her on my lap, and explained the situation to her while she sniffled.

I learned something about myself today. I'm willing to let Alleke make her own mistakes, as long as they don't carry a hefty price tag. I would rather have her make her mistakes now when the stakes are low than later in life when she may face major consequences for her actions.

Come to think of it, I could have benefited from falling off a bench when I was a toddler. When I was in Middle School I jumped out of a tree house to see if it would hurt when I hit the ground.

I cried too.

1 YEAR, 2 MONTHS, 5 DAYS
Rocking Horse

Alleke stood next to me and watched as I hung the last ornament on the tree, then I reached over the back of the couch and plugged in the lights.

The corner of the room danced like a hundred fireflies, especially after April got up and turned off the rest of the lights in the apartment, at which point Alleke turned to me, scrunched up her nose, and belly laughed.

Alleke pointed at a rocking horse made of felt hanging on a low branch. She walked over and picked it off the tree, studied it, and handed it to me. Then she walked back to the tree and reached for another. She looked over her shoulder to see if I would help her.

I smiled, hung the rocking horse back on the tree, and lifted Alleke into my lap. I explained that we look at Christmas ornaments, but we don't touch them. I set Alleke back down in front of the tree to see if she understood. She stared at the tree for a while, figured something out, then walked away and busied herself with one of the books lying on the floor in front of her toy cupboard.

Wow, that was easier than I thought it would be, I thought to myself. I reached for my cup of hot chocolate and took a sip.

The next morning April and Alleke had friends coming over, so I picked up around the apartment. Our bedroom doubles as my office, and the floor was covered with scrap paper. Alleke had discovered the stack under the printer and pulled it apart by throwing sheets in the air to see where they would land.

I had the room mostly picked up, but I thought I better check under the bed just in case. I got down on my knees and pulled up the bed covers. I could see a few dust bunnies, and sure enough, sheets of scrap paper scattered all the way to the backside of the bed.

I also found something I didn't know I was missing. It was a Christmas ornament. Actually, it was a little rocking horse made of felt.

1 YEAR, 2 MONTHS, 26 DAYS
Accomplice

I was peeling a clementine when Alleke slid a book onto the table next to me. It was *Lord of the Flies*.

I glanced over at the bookshelf and found the slot, like a missing tooth, on the second shelf. I sighed.

"This is not Alleke's book," I explained again, holding up the book. "It's daddy's book." I handed it to her.

"Can you put it back on the shelf please?" I asked. I pointed at the slot on the second shelf.

Alleke dutifully carried the book over to the shelf and laid it on top of the other books.

"Thanks," I said. I busied myself again with peeling and eating my clementine, and it wasn't until I finished that I heard Alleke pouting. I looked up.

She was at the bookshelf again, and this time she had Brian, her Cabbage Patch Kid. She was holding Brian up so he could reach the books on the second shelf. If she couldn't take books from the shelf, maybe he could.

The problem was Brian wasn't cooperating, and Alleke was getting frustrated. She whined some more and pressed Brian as hard as she could into the books on the shelf.

"Alleke," I said softly.

She froze, dropped Brian in front of the bookshelf, ran over, and stood next to me.

She looked at me and pointed at Brian, as if to say, "He did it."

1 YEAR, 3 MONTHS, 1 DAY
Pickpocket

I was at the same Ecuadorian restaurant—the one that's decorated like a pirate ship—eating a fried banana and talking with friends when I happened to glance over and notice that Alleke had squatted down next to the table and was pulling money and credit cards out of an open wallet.

I looked around the room.

"Um...did someone give Alleke a wallet to play with because

it and taking out all the money and credit

ible looked at each other.

I said, dangling the wallet like a snake by

tri?" someone asked at the other end of

here," Terri said. Everyone watched as
e for a while, then stopped and looked
asked. She squinted across the table.

up the pile of coins, bills and cards
them to their compartments in the wallet. She knew
out where everything belonged, and when we finished, I asked
her politely to put the wallet back where she had found it.

Alleke led me around to the far side of the table, dropped
the wallet in Terri's bag, which was hanging off her chair, and
smiled. I could see that she was proud of herself for doing what
she was told.

I don't know why I was surprised. We live in the city after
all, where everyone has a story about a wallet or an iPod or a
bag that was stolen and a theory about who took it when. I had
overlooked, perhaps, the most basic question about right and
wrong in Alleke's world.

So, I sat down next to her and began to explain.

"Honey," I said, "we don't steal people's wallets."

1 YEAR, 4 MONTHS, 6 DAYS

Cooking Together

"Not now," I said, wincing. I finished chopping the red
onion and set it aside.

Alleke stood at my feet and reached for me to pick her up.

When that didn't work, she wedged her way between my legs and the counter and began pushing me out of the kitchen.

I set the knife down, kneeled, and looked Alleke in the eyes. "Look," I said, "I can't hold you and cook at the same time." I leaned in and gave her a kiss. "You're going to have to wait until I'm finished."

Alleke frowned, sat back on her haunches like a weightlifter, and began to howl.

I was cutting around the stem of a red pepper when April walked into the kitchen to see what was the matter. She didn't say anything, just looked down at Alleke, all crumpled up like a discarded soda can, then scanned the room until she found what she was looking for, a small wooden step stool. She dragged the stool across the floor until it was in front of the dishwasher next to me. April picked up our ball of tears, gave her a kiss on the back of the neck, and set her on top of the stool. Then she left.

Alleke whimpered some more, and then she was quiet. She cocked her head and peered up at me.

I smiled.

She whimpered again, and then as if someone had pulled the string on a lawnmower, she erupted into laughter, her whole body rattling. It took a minute before she calmed down enough to stand up and look around.

I reached across the counter for a bag of green beans and set them down in front of her. "I need your help," I said. I opened the bag and pulled out a small handful of beans. "These need to go in the sink, so we can wash them," I added, "like this," and I tossed the handful into the sink.

Alleke looked up at me and giggled. Then, she stood on her tippy toes, reached across the counter, and shoved her hand into the bag.

1 YEAR, 4 MONTHS, 22 DAYS
Toothbrush

"Open up," I said. I leaned over the changing table with the miniature toothbrush and aimed it at Alleke's mouth. She pushed it aside with both hands, turned over, and lifted herself up on all fours—all at once like a tumbling gymnast.

"Nigh nigh," she said, suggesting we skip this part of our nighttime ritual. She reached for me to pick her up.

I glared at her and crossed my arms. "No way," I said. "You're mean." I contemplated sticking out my tongue.

This was the third night in a row that Alleke had refused to brush her teeth, and first time she had decided not to do something I couldn't make her do. I could not brush her teeth without her help. It was impossible.

I entertained the idea of not brushing Alleke's teeth anymore. I'd wave the toothbrush in her face, then toss it in the wastebasket. "You'll see," I'd say. Years later she would have rotten teeth like pieces of broken glass, and it would be her fault, not mine.

I shuddered at the thought.

"What should I do?" I asked April, who had been listening to our conversation from the couch in the living room.

April looked up from her laptop and thought for a moment. "Let her brush your teeth," she said.

I dug around in the drawer until I found my toothbrush and handed it to Alleke. She giggled and immediately pointed it at my mouth. As if following orders from my dentist, I opened wide, and she went to work scrubbing my teeth. Laughing didn't help. It made the process more difficult for both of us, but we couldn't stop.

When Alleke finished, she set down my toothbrush and pointed at the miniature one in my hand.

I aimed the little toothbrush at her mouth and said, "Open up."

1 YEAR, 5 MONTHS, 11 DAYS

Prayer

The first time I had contemplated Alleke's spirituality was at the dinner table. She was staring at me from her high chair while I prayed, and I realized that although I had no idea how to make God make sense to a 5-month-old—let alone myself most of the time—Alleke was still watching me, and she wanted to know what I was doing.

My first thought was to teach her to fold her hands while we prayed. But, I couldn't remember what folding our hands had to do with God. Maybe it was a way to keep kids' hands quiet? Then I thought of other families I knew like Byron and Lisa and their kids who held hands around the table when they prayed. I liked that. Holding hands suggested trust, togetherness and hospitality.

So, April and I decided we would hold hands while we prayed, but we also decided we wouldn't make Alleke hold hands with us if she didn't want to. We would extend a hand to her, and if she wanted to join in, she could.

I guess the idea of making Alleke hold hands with us seemed to miss the point. Praying wasn't about holding hands. It wasn't about doing something, but choosing something. It was choosing to take time out of our day to be together and thank God for providing for us.

Prayer, like a hug or a kiss, was an outward expression of something we felt inside.

I'll admit that extending Alleke a hand was ridiculous at first.

Alleke wasn't old enough, so she didn't understand what we were doing. Almost a year went by, and nothing happened, except that somewhere along the way I forgot to hope that Alleke might actually choose to join us in prayer.

Then one day I was praying as usual with my open hand resting on the table next to Alleke, and I felt her little fingers slip inside mine like a glove. When I finished and opened my eyes, I noticed that April was holding her other hand.

"Did you do that?" I asked April. I nodded at Alleke's hand in hers.

April shook her head and smiled. "I guess it felt right to her today," April said.

Nowadays Alleke prays with us every day. Sometimes she even makes us pray twice or three times during a meal, and she never misses an opportunity to say "Maymen."

I've learned something about myself too. Usually the parts of life that are the most important to me are also the parts that I refuse to make Alleke do. I suppose I can't bear the thought of taking away from her the choices that were so important to me.

1 YEAR, 5 MONTHS, 17 DAYS

Columbus

Alleke stood at the front door and pointed. I couldn't help but notice her resemblance to the monument of Christopher Columbus in Barcelona pointing the way to the Americas. Ironically, the statue points towards Italy, not the New World, which gave me an idea. My plan had been to take Alleke down to the playground, but now I was curious to find out where she would take me. She would lead, and I would follow.

I grabbed my keys off the table and opened the door. Alleke raced over to the elevator and waited for me to push the button.

When the doors opened on the ground floor, she dangled from my hand as we took the steps. I yanked at the heavy wooden door until it opened, and Alleke ran out into the street.

She was nearly at the corner before I got hold of her hand, like grabbing a dog by the collar. Actually, the experience was a lot like walking a dog. Alleke would stop to look at something like a cigarette butt on the sidewalk, then prance along ahead of me, never once in a straight line of course, but always back and forth like she was hiking up a mountain. She tired quickly, so I scooped her up in my arms. Now she was the captain, and I was the ship.

"Where do we go now?" I asked at the next corner, wondering if she actually knew where she was going, or if she always pointed at what was in front of her.

She pointed to my right.

I smiled as we turned the corner and began walking down towards the playground. At every corner I asked her the way, and every time she assured me it was straight ahead. When we got to the square with the playground at the other end, she unbuckled herself from my arms like a seat belt and dashed off across the cobblestones, scattering pigeons.

I caught up with her again, and this time she was chatting with an elderly woman who wanted to know her name and asked if her hair was really that blonde or if her parents had dyed it that way. Alleke politely answered all her questions, but in a language neither the elderly woman nor I were familiar with.

In the end, Alleke didn't make it to the playground. Instead, she climbed up on a park bench and watched dogs chase rubber balls. I suppose that's what explorers do. They chart their course, but if they find something else more interesting along the way—say the Americas, instead of a shortcut to India—they're willing to recognize that the process of discovery is always more important than the final destination.

Lessons from Africa

Byron and Lisa are some friends of ours who live in Tanzania, and for many years lived among the Maasai people in Kenya. For a short time, they lived with their kids in Portugal where April and I would visit them once a year before Alleke was born. They would invite us into their family for a few days, and we would spend most evenings around the fireplace with a cup of tea listening to them tell stories from Africa.

Of course I remember the story about the house they built in the jungle burning to the ground. I remember the story about children in their village being paralyzed by a local witch doctor. I remember the one about Byron's favorite dog, a Jack Russell Terrier, which is a small dog with a lot of courage, breaking his neck trying to protect Byron from a leopard.

For as many memorable stories as they told us, I'm surprised one story in particular sticks with me more than the others. I use this story almost every day as a parent.

Lisa explained to us one afternoon while her daughter was helping her in the kitchen that where they had lived in Africa children didn't really have toys. Instead, they spent most of their time pretending to do the same household tasks as their parents. So while mom was building a fire, her daughter might gather some sticks and also pretend to build a fire. A child's play was not defined by toys, but by curiosity and imagination.

I find this perspective on play helpful for a number of reasons. For one, it means we can play anytime anywhere, even if we don't have toys (or kids). As long as we bring our curiosity and imagination, something as mundane as sorting the recycling or grocery shopping can be playtime.

Secondly, play is not limited to toys, which is a relief to me because I don't actually like most toys. I get bored, which makes me feel like an uninterested parent. I remind myself that I can be playful, even without Play-Doh or building blocks. Alleke loves splashing around in the kitchen sink while I'm making meals, and yesterday she couldn't wait to go up on the roof to help April pot new plants.

Finally, engaging in play while we do our housework is developmental. In our case, it teaches Alleke how to do our household chores herself and demonstrates that they can be done playfully.

Work and play can be one and the same, and I hope Alleke learns that from me—because actually, I do whistle while I work.

1 YEAR, 7 MONTHS
Puddle

Laura bounded away from the cabin into the tall grass, then stopped. She looked up and squinted. "I think it's starting to rain," she said, looking back at me.

I watched as the clouds appeared to break over the mountains like river rapids, rushing down into the valley and pooling over our heads.

I put up my umbrella.

I didn't want to get wet, but I had no intention of returning to the city without going for a hike first. Alleke was on my back, and I felt I owed it to her to see for herself that what lay beyond the city was not empty, but full of life too.

I grew up with cows grazing in my backyard, and I couldn't bear the thought that for Alleke farm animals were mythical creatures that only existed in books. As far as she was concerned, a chicken was as plausible as a Zizzer-Zazzer-Zuzz, one of Dr. Seuss' beasts with a pink mop for hair and a checkerboard body.

So, I led the way to the front gate, and we set off downhill looking for signs of life.

By the time we reached the edge of the village, the rain had stopped, and we found ourselves hopping over puddles as we followed a cattle path through emerald pastures. While April was holding Alleke, we came upon a trickling stream where I was the first to notice three tall horses standing along the bank munching on grass.

I ran ahead to point at the horses, and immediately April set Alleke down so she could come over and see them. Alleke sat there giggling excitedly and doing her jumping jacks before she finally dashed off after us. She was so curious, and so focused that she didn't notice the first silvery puddle in front of her. She plunged in and splashed around, then her boot stuck, she lost her balance, and she fell in the mud. When April and I reached her, she was still lying in the mud, not sure what to do. April lifted her into her arms, and Alleke sobbed and held out her hands for me to see. They were covered in a layer of mud as thick and creamy as chocolate frosting.

We didn't pay much attention to the horses after that. Thankfully April had a tissue to wipe off Alleke's hands. We pulled off her pants, which were sopping wet, and I managed to fold them up in such a way that I could stuff them in my back pocket without getting myself too wet.

We did keep walking, and we saw cows, and chickens, a goat, a donkey, and eventually when we made our way back, we even saw storks nested on top of the small church in the village.

I guess you could say Alleke was initiated into life as a kid in the country. The first rule I learned as a kid about playing outside was the dirtier I got, the more fun I had.

1 YEAR, 8 MONTHS, 7 DAYS

Socks

I've always thought April was strange for using her socks to clean things. I'm not talking about old socks with holes in them that have been retired to the pile of rags. I'm talking about the ones she's wearing at any given moment.

For example, I remember taking April to The Olive Garden when we had been dating for about a year. She had some tomato sauce on her finger, so she reached down and wiped it on her sock, like that was the most normal thing to do, even though she had a napkin on her lap.

On another occasion we volunteered to paint a church in Kalamazoo, Michigan where we were living for the summer. When we finished for the day, April sat down on the front step and wiped her hands off on her socks. I still see the fingerprints on that pair of socks when they go through the wash.

If April were here to speak for herself, she would say that wiping things on her socks is better than wiping them on her sleeve because socks go in the wash at the end of the day, and most of the time no one sees her socks anyway. I can't argue with her there, and really, what's more convenient than having a rag or a napkin on your foot, always at your disposal?

Anyway, the reason I'm telling you all of this is because today we had spaghetti for lunch. Alleke doesn't eat spaghetti. She puts her face in the bowl and sucks up each noodle like a vacuum. When she's finished, she looked like a clown with a tomato-sauce grin.

I shouldn't have been surprised by what Alleke did next. She doesn't like having a messy face, so she reached down under her high chair, pulled off one of her socks, politely wiped the spaghetti sauce off her face with the sock, and then pulled the sock on again.

She pushed her bowl across the table to me and said, "All done daddy."

1 YEAR, 8 MONTHS, 23 DAYS
Guitar Case

I was sitting on the couch playing guitar when I heard the bathroom door open. Alleke scampered into the room looking for music like a kid after an ice cream truck. She had escaped from the bathtub, which made my music her victory song as she giggled and galloped circles around the room.

Much later after Alleke had exhausted herself with spinning in circles, she crawled into my guitar case with a blanket and closed her eyes.

I strummed a lullaby.

It wasn't until after she sat up, got out, and began running around again that I noticed the little puddle in the bottom of my case.

1 YEAR, 9 MONTHS, 12 DAYS
Potty Training

Potty training was Alleke's idea. She came streaking through the apartment, dripping from her inflatable swimming pool in the kitchen. I watched her hop like a dolphin with her knees together and disappear into the bathroom.

"Potty," she yelled, and I bolted out of my chair.

Alleke sat on her potty and kicked her legs while I sat on the edge of the tub—not sure if I was supposed to do something.

I had as much experience with potty training as Alleke did. She seemed confident at least.

Alleke asked to read a book, and when she finished, she set it down, stood up, looked in the potty, and pointed. I looked over her shoulder.

There was a puddle.

"Nice work," I said.

I'm no expert on potty training. Alleke just lets me tag along when she has to go. I'm there for moral support. But what I find interesting is that Alleke started using the potty when she had to.

It's been hot, so Alleke's been running around in her birthday suit, in and out of her pool like our apartment is her personal water park. Alleke had a few accidents at first, one involving a turd rolling under the couch, but once she realized diapers were no longer an option, she looked for the next best thing, the toilet, which she had seen Mom and Dad use. Potty training was not so much an accomplishment, like crossing a finish line, but a solution to a problem. It was practical.

Let's just hope Alleke doesn't realize the easier option would be to go in her swimming pool.

1 YEAR, 9 MONTHS, 19 DAYS

Imagination

Alleke picked up a breadcrumb off the table, dropped it on the floor, and leaned over to see where it had fallen.

"Here doggie," she said, "food," and pointed at the crumb.

April and I looked at each other. We didn't own a dog.

I peered under the table and looked for something that might have reminded Alleke of a dog. I didn't see anything, only more crumbs.

"Doggie, food!" Alleke shouted impatiently. She picked up another crumb and tossed it.

April and I watched Alleke feed the dog some more, as if we were playing charades and Alleke was acting out the same word or phrase until we guessed what it was. April finally guessed right. "I think she's using her imagination," she said.

I suppose it seems obvious that kids use their imaginations. Most of us return to our childhoods to think of a time when we used our imaginations. Still, not all kids use their imaginations—not the smallest ones. The ability to imagine is something that's developed over time, which meant that up until now Alleke had been a very literal, concrete person. She could remember something that had happened to her, but she couldn't imagine a hypothetical situation, something that hadn't happened, but could have happened.

April and I were so used to Alleke only talking about things that were actually real that when Alleke said she was feeding the dog, I looked under the table.

So I started to play along. I broke the end off the baguette and pretended to feed the dog under the table by tearing off pieces and hiding them, then showing Alleke what was left so it actually looked like the dog was eating the bread.

Alleke's eyes went wide. She stood up in her high chair and pointed at what was left in my hand. "Doggie, doggie," she chanted. She reached for me to set her down on the ground and ran around the table looking for the dog.

That's when I realized we weren't imagining anymore. Alleke had only begun learning how to imagine, and somehow in the process of me feeding the dog, the dog had become real. She thought I was actually feeding a dog.

I sighed. I didn't know how to break it to Alleke that there was no dog under the table.

"Doggie?" Alleke asked innocently, holding out her hands.

"Um...he's sleeping," I said and bit my lip.

I wasn't lying. I was using my imagination.

Obsession

Alleke sat quietly on April's lap when the lights went off and everyone began to sing. It wasn't until after the cake went up in smoke and the room filled with laughter that Alleke lunged for her mom's neck.

If you had asked me, I would have told you Alleke was terrified of her mom's birthday, but the next day she had a tea party with her dollies and sang, "Ahhpppy Birrrday t'MAMA."

That was only the beginning. "The Happy Birthday Song" would become Alleke's first notable obsession, and it was fascinating to see how she could create an entire empire of associations around this one song, simply by linking one experience to another, then grouping them, and forming meaning. After some time, virtually every person or place or thing reminded Alleke of the "The Happy Birthday Song," and she would break into song yet again.

Alleke's obsession started with cakes and candles, but soon anything that looked like a candle would do, even crayons or ChapStick or street lamps. Flowers reminded Alleke of birthdays because flowers were sitting on the table at her mom's birthday party. Music in general reminded Alleke of birthdays. She would beg to watch birthday videos on YouTube, especially the video of her sitting on her mom's lap with her face glowing over all those candles. Alleke would watch the video over and over, and she would cry when the time came to do something else.

"The Happy Birthday Song" was more than a tune with lyrics, it was a worldview, a lens by which Alleke interpreted her surroundings, or maybe a creed, something she could use to judge her experiences and give them meaning. When she got bored, she would sing the song. When she wanted to give someone a compliment, she would sing the song and fill in the blank with his or her name. Sometimes I would wake in the middle of the night to Alleke singing the song in her sleep, no doubt rehearsing another birthday in her dreams. When she finally saw her Uncle Rick in person and had difficulty pronouncing his name, she elected to refer to him by singing the song, since we had recently celebrated his birthday. Rick's name was "The Happy Birthday Song."

At first I didn't know what to make of Alleke's obsession. I didn't like celebrating our birthdays every day because I thought our birthdays wouldn't seem as special when they actually happened. But I changed my mind because really, who doesn't want every day to be a birthday.

That's the difference between adults and kids. Adults say we can't, and kids say we can. Adults say only some days are special, or more accurately, only some people are special on some days. It's all very complicated and requires a calendar and some forethought.

For kids, every day is special, and every person is special every day. Alleke likes to remind me of this by telling me today is my birthday too, and that for me is worth singing about.

1 YEAR, 10 MONTHS
Bubbles

April stood at the corner of the playground and blew bubbles. Alleke stood next to her and watched as one little girl left her shovel in the sand and started swatting at the small, crystal planets hovering in orbit over their heads. Two little boys on the teeter totter noticed next and came running. Before long, the playground was a frenzy of boys and girls chasing bubbles like they chase butterflies—jumping, swatting, diving, and twirling. It was a mosh pit for toddlers.

Alleke giggled at the others, then barreled into a cloud of bubbles, shrieking like she had sprung a leak.

April blew bubbles until the bottle ran out. I was surprised the kids lasted that long, and they weren't convinced the bubbles were gone until April let them see the empty bottle. April put the lid back on, and the kids began to walk away.

Alleke ran over. She looked at April, then at the kids, then at the bottle. "Open, open, open," she pleaded. She took the bottle and tried to get the cap off. When it wouldn't budge, she began to cry. Most of the kids, it seemed, had gone home for dinner, and now the playground was empty.

Bringing bubbles to the playground was Alleke's idea in the first place. She loves playing with other kids, but most of the time she just stands there and watches them play. She observes. She seems fascinated with kids, not comfortable with them. If Alleke is playing on the slide and kids get in line behind her, she steps aside and waits for them to finish. She doesn't seem confident in what she's doing.

I worry Alleke is learning my bad habits. She's hesitant at the playground because I am. I don't feel like I belong there. I'm still not sure what the unwritten rules are at the playground, so I hang back. The other parents seem to know each other, so I sit and watch them talk.

I don't feel like I can be myself at the playground, not yet.

Alleke may not feel like herself either, but she did bring bubbles to the playground. She brought something she likes to play with at home to the playground so she could share it with the other kids—and it worked. Even though her way of connecting with the kids might not have been the expected way, she still found a way.

1 YEAR, 10 MONTHS, 4 DAYS
Preschool

A little boy and girl were shoveling sand into cups and serving them as lemon ice cream to anyone who walked past the playground. I pointed the kids out to Alleke, who was perched on a swing, and asked if she wanted to play with them.

Alleke always says yes when I ask her if she wants to play with other kids. The only condition is I have to come too. So, I followed her over to the ice cream parlor where the little boy and girl were garnishing their cups of ice cream with dried leaves. I helped Alleke find a place to sit between them and showed her a plastic scoop she could use.

Alleke studied the situation for a moment, then got up, took a few steps back, and sat down again, far enough away that she didn't have to play with the little boy and girl, but she could still watch them.

This summer hasn't turned out exactly how I had hoped. Next week we'll be at a conference in Hungary, and then we'll repack our suitcases and leave again with our friends David and Daphne for a family vacation on the beach. We've either been traveling or hosting guests all summer, and Alleke hasn't had the opportunity to go to the playground on a regular basis and develop significant relationships with the kids there. As a result, I often feel like a dad on a leash. The other parents chat on benches around the perimeter of the playground while their kids run off to play, and then there's me, chasing Alleke. I've always loved the fact that Alleke wants to play with her daddy, but recently I've begun to wonder if I'm actually stopping her from playing with her peers.

While my Dutch friend Marlies pointed out that Alleke might just be shy and that's okay, I also want to make sure that I've given Alleke enough opportunities to be a social person if that's who she is. It would be one thing if Alleke was always around other kids, and she was still shy, but it's another thing if she's a social person, but feels awkward around other kids because she simply hasn't had the chance to get to know them and learn how to play with them. Alleke doesn't have siblings, she spends most of her time with her parents, and her parents don't have many friends who have kids, so she doesn't have the opportunity to interact with other kids very often.

So, April and I are thinking about sending Alleke to preschool. We hadn't considered preschool before since we had made the decision to have one of us home at all times to care for Alleke. However, our current lifestyle doesn't give Alleke the opportunity to play with a group of kids on a regular basis and build friendships. If we could find a preschool where Alleke could go maybe three mornings a week, that would be ideal.

A handful of nuns run a preschool in an old stone convent on the square down the street. My friend Joe used to send his daughter there, so I'll give him a call this morning and ask a few questions.

In the meantime, I'll try to give Alleke a little more space at the playground.

1 YEAR, 10 MONTHS, 7 DAYS

Nursery

Balancing a cup of tea, I excused my way through the tangle of people and chairs and sat down in the empty seat next to April. Alleke was hanging around her neck.

I leaned over. "What's Alleke doing here?" I whispered while a man in front gave announcements from a microphone.

"She didn't want to stay in the nursery," April whispered back.

I thought for a moment.

"I'm not sure Alleke gets to make that decision," I said. "We've paid a lot of money to be at this conference so we could be in these sessions without being distracted by our daughter."

April frowned. "I'm not going to leave Alleke in a strange place if she doesn't want to stay there," she said.

I rubbed my forehead. April had a point. I wouldn't want to be left in a room full of strangers either, especially without anyone I knew. The situation would be completely different if Alleke already knew someone in the nursery. Still...

"We're always talking about how Alleke doesn't have any friends her age. The nursery is full of kids her age. The sooner she spends time there, the sooner she'll make friends she can play with the rest of the week. She'll be uncomfortable at first, but the experience will be good for her."

April took the diaper bag from the table and handed it to me.

"You do it then," she said. She undid Alleke's arms from around her neck and dropped Alleke in my lap.

"Mama," Alleke cried. As I stood up, Alleke tried to break free, her screams muffling the speaker's words as effectively as if I had run from the room banging a pot with a wooden spoon.

No wonder Alleke doesn't like me as much as her mom, I thought, as we left the building and crossed the grass to the playground. I'm mean.

I set Alleke down on the gravel, and as if drawn by some magnetic force, her feet carried her off towards the teeter-totter where a few kids were pushing it up and down like an oil rig. I stood there for a while waiting for Alleke to notice that she had left me. Eventually I gave up and wandering back into the building. When I found my seat, I leaned over and whispered again in April's ear.

"She didn't even notice me leave."

April nodded.

"I still think I was right," she whispered back.

"So, does that mean you think I was wrong?" I snapped back.

"No."

I thought about that for a second.

"Isn't that a contradiction?" I asked.

"I don't think it has to be."

1 YEAR, 10 MONTHS, 9 DAYS

Baby Monitor

The waiter came over and started gathering our dishes.

"I'm going to run up to our room and wake up Alleke," I said. I chugged my orange juice and pushed my chair away from the table.

"Don't forget the baby monitor," April said as she pointed at the box with the antenna sitting quietly among the dishes.

I grabbed the monitor. "I'm surprised she's still asleep," I said.

As I walked to the elevators, the monitor began to static like a radio between stations. Then, as if someone was working the dial and found a signal, the monitor surged and the room flooded with the swells of a wailing toddler.

"Alleke!" I cried.

I ran for the stairs, bounded up them, and crashed through the door into the hallway on the fourth floor.

One of the housekeeping staff was standing in the hallway holding Alleke in her arms. Alleke had one arm around her blankie, the other around the woman's neck, and she was sniffling.

The woman walked over and put Alleke in my arms. She said something in Hungarian, which perhaps wasn't even intended for me, then walked back down the hall, picked up a stack of towels from her cart, and disappeared in a room.

"Thank you," I yelled after her as I held Alleke's head against my chest.

1 YEAR, 10 MONTHS, 29 DAYS
Motion Sickness

Shani wrenched the steering wheel and bumbled off the highway towards a gas station. She brought the car to a screeching halt, the doors sprung open, and all six of us scrambled out—as if the car were swarming with bees.

Alleke had vomited in the car. She was too young to know how to use the paper bag in front of her, so she had fought the car seat and swung her head around like a loose garden hose, retching all over herself, the seats, and those of us trying to help her. The backseat looked like a paintball park, my nose burned from the smell of ammonia, and Alleke was screaming hysterically, no doubt horrified that her body had gone into reverse.

One of the side effects of living in the city without a car, we've discovered, is motion sickness. April laments how she used to be able to ride in a car backwards reading a book for hours without a problem. Now, because she goes everywhere on foot, even the thought of getting in a car makes her stomach turn.

After that trip, we abandoned our car seat at a friend's house. We just left it there on their porch without even washing it. Six months passed. Then, a couple weeks before we left for the conference in Hungary, our friends David and Daphne asked if we wanted to take a road trip to Valencia—in their car—and we said yes. We couldn't avoid cars forever.

The day before our road trip, we stopped by to pick up the car seat, wash it out, and take it home. While we stood in front of our apartment building and I dug around in my pockets for keys, Alleke held up her hand and said, "*No casa.*"

"You don't want to go home?" I asked.

"Where do you want to go?" April probed.

"Broom broom," Alleke replied, her chin up, pointing at the car seat sitting on the sidewalk.

I raised an eyebrow.

"You want to go in a broom broom," I said, as condescendingly as if she had asked me to buy her a pony. "Do you remember the last time you rode in a broom broom?"

Alleke nodded and giggled. "Broom broom," she said.

April and I spent the rest of the day explaining a new concept to Alleke called "tomorrow." Just when I thought Alleke understood she had to go "night night" before she could get in the car, she walked over and started dragging the car seat towards the front door, stopping occasionally to point at the door and say, "Broom broom."

The car trip to Valencia went fine. Alleke is finally old enough to take Dramamine, so she slept most of the way. I'm sitting here at the beach scribbling these words down in a notebook while I watch April and Alleke scamper back and forth down the beach collecting shells. Now that we're here, I think I'm beginning to understand why Alleke wanted to get in that car seat, even though it made her sick before.

Alleke has learned that getting in a car means being together as a family. It means she has Mom and Dad all to herself, and finally she gets all the attention she wants. It means Mom and Dad don't have to go to work. It means she gets to play all day. Ultimately, I think it means Alleke weighed the costs of getting sick again and decided it was still worth it to her to get in the car.

Parents make sacrifices for their kids, and sometimes, kids make sacrifices for their parents.

I Scream. You Scream. We all Scream for Ice Cream.

Alleke screams now. It all began over a piece of birthday cake. I got the last one, topped with vanilla ice cream, and sat down on the couch to eat it when Alleke noticed me take my first bite. Immediately she was at my side standing on her tippy toes and peering into my dish.

I was hesitant to share. I'll admit it. I mean it was my birthday cake, and I was the one who had slaved away for an entire morning to make it, and well, this was the last piece.

I took another bite and expected Alleke to do what she always does, which is to cock her head like a puppy, smile big for the camera, and ask politely, "Ice keem, peas?" Instead, she clinched her fists, pressed her eyes shut, and screamed.

A scream is so much more than noise. It's unfiltered emotion. It's like popping the hood and listening to the engine roar inside of us. For a brief moment, it tells us what's going on inside someone, and almost always, we're startled by what we hear.

Alleke wanted ice cream, but instead of asking, this time she screamed because something had changed about her. The untamed creature inside of her called her "will," which was not bound by reason or virtue, had finally been freed from its cage. Her will was a wild beast, roaming around inside of her and howling at the moon.

At bedtime I asked Alleke if I could brush her teeth, and she screamed in my face. I told her the sooner we brushed her teeth, the sooner she could have her blankie and read books, but I guess it was too important to her to sit there at the edge of her changing table holding her toothbrush and shrieking. So, I left her there. I came back a couple times to check on her, and she was still exercising her lungs. Eventually I lied and told her I was going to bed. I said "Night night," turned off the lights, and left her in the dark.

"Daddy?" I heard her ask quietly.

Sometimes I find it so difficult not to get mad at Alleke when she screams. I end up yelling at her for yelling at me. It's like trying to make peace in the Middle East with big guns. I'm such an emotional person that she gets me going immediately. I can only imagine what it's going to be like when she's a teenager. We won't need words, only foghorns.

I can't help feeling like we're starting over again as parents. Up until now we've relied on Alleke to tell us what she needed. We trusted that when she cried, she needed something. When she said she was hungry, she was hungry. When she looked tired, it was time for her nap. We took our cues from her. But that's not working anymore because of this wild beast that's loose inside her. Now Alleke not only needs things, she wants things too. She relies less on her instinct, and more on her will, and she's actually making decisions for herself. Some of her decisions are terrible, and April and I need to help her learn how to make good decisions.

Alleke's metamorphosis caught me so off guard I actually dug through some boxes under our bed until I found my old Developmental Psychology textbook from college. I found this interesting part in the book about Erik Erikson's stages of psychosocial development. Basically, this guy says life can be boiled down to a series of eight challenges. At each stage of life, we need to overcome a specific challenge. For a newborn, the challenge is trusting her parents, and by extension, the world around her. She wants to know if her needs will be met and if her parents care for her. Erikson calls this challenge "Trust vs. Mistrust."

In the second challenge, a toddler realizes for the first time that she's an individual, and she is capable of making decisions for herself. This challenge is called "Autonomy vs. Shame and Doubt." By exercising her will in all kinds of different situations, she learns that she can make good decisions with positive outcomes or bad decisions that carry consequences. She can do some things for herself, and for the rest she can rely on others like Mom and Dad to help her. I looked up from the book. Adolescence had started earlier than I expected, and for a brief moment I imagined an independent Alleke backpacking through the jungles of Peru with dreadlocks and an eyebrow piercing.

The point was Alleke wasn't acting up, she was acting her age. She was supposed to start screaming now in the same way puppies are supposed to pee all over the floor—until you train them. Alleke needed to be trained too, and well, that's about as far as I've gotten in my thinking.

For now, the only thing I was certain about was Alleke wasn't getting any of my birthday cake.

1 YEAR, 11 MONTHS, 3 DAYS
No Yes

Alleke lay sobbing on the floor in the living room while April stood in the doorway to the kitchen eating pizza dough off her fingers.

"Alleke," April said. "Guess what we're having for dinner?"
Alleke lifted her head.

"It's your favorite," April said, giving her a hint.

Alleke frowned.

"We're having pizza for dinner," April said, as excitedly as if she had announced we were going to Disneyland for Christmas.

Alleke shook her head. "No yes," she screamed.

April looked at me. "What does that mean?"

"No yes," Alleke cried and buried her face in her hands.

I picked Alleke up off the floor and tickled her until she began to giggle.

"I think she means no and yes," I said. "No, because toddlers don't agree with their parents out of principle. Yes, because she really does want pizza. It's her favorite food."

1 YEAR, 11 MONTHS, 4 DAYS

Blue Marker

Alleke and I were jumping on the bed and playing balloon volleyball, which is what we do every day when April is gone, when Alleke noticed something on the bottom of her foot. She sat down on the bed to inspect it. I peered over her shoulder at the fuzzy blue spot on her heel, then noticed the ribbon of blue ink running up her calf and across her thigh. She even had blue fingertips.

Alleke was so upset by the blue spot on the bottom of her foot that she started limping in circles on the bed and howling because of the imaginary pain. I tried to convince her that the blue spot on her foot was not an owie, but as soon as I mentioned the word, she wailed even harder, blubbering till she was bubbling at the mouth.

I managed to console her by putting a small band-aid over

the spot, which only reinforced her belief that the blue spot was actually doing her some harm.

However, with the band-aid in place, Alleke happily limped around the house after me while I looked for the source of the blue spot. If Alleke was covered in blue ink, what else would be blue? I also wondered how she had managed to find the time to cover herself in blue ink when she had not been out of sight all morning.

I was even more puzzled after looking around the house. Everything was as it should be. No blue ink anywhere. Eventually I found the blue marker, which strangely enough was capped securely in the art drawer.

If nothing else, the blue spot on the bottom of Alleke's foot was a good reminder that I don't know everything about my daughter, even though I might think I do.

April and I talked last night, and we've decided to send Alleke to preschool in the mornings when she turns three. As much as we've tried to make changes, our lifestyle hasn't given Alleke the opportunity to make friends her age. It seems unfair that all of her friends are college graduates.

So, even though I can't imagine dropping Alleke off at preschool and leaving her there, the reality is, the older she gets, the less control I will have over her life. The goal isn't to keep an eye on Alleke every time she plays with markers, but to train her to make wise decisions for herself even when no one is looking.

1 YEAR, 11 MONTHS, 5 DAYS
Politically Correct

Alleke crawled to the end of her bed and switched off the lamp, then found her blankie and buried her face in her pillow.

I knelt down next to her bed and began softly singing a lullaby.

> Hush-a-bye, don't you cry.
> Go to sleepy, little baby.

Alleke sat up in bed. "Daddy?" she asked.

"Yes," I said.

"Alleke no baby," she said. "Alleke girl."

I thought for a moment and tried to make sense of what she was saying. She usually spoke in riddles, like Jesus.

"Alleke's not a baby anymore. She's a girl?" I asked, taking a shot in the dark.

Alleke nodded excitedly.

"So, you don't want me to sing lullabies about babies anymore?" I asked.

Alleke nodded again, this time bouncing up and down on her bed.

I laughed.

"As you wish," I said. "No more lullabies about babies. Only lullabies about little girls."

Once again Alleke snuggled up with her pillow and pulled her blankie close to her chest.

I took a deep breath and began again.

> Hush-a-bye, don't you cry.
> Go to sleepy little girl...

1 YEAR, 11 MONTHS, 8 DAYS

Funeral

I walked down the steps of the church, across the lawn, and passed through the scattered headstones to the plot of black dirt. My grandpa had been buried here on Wednesday.

The wind beat against me, and I shivered and crossed my arms. I marveled at how everything, including the fields of bronzed cornstalks already harvested and left to be chopped, was a metaphor for life and death when it came time to say goodbye.

My dad had left a message on my answering machine on Sunday saying Grandpa had quietly passed away that morning in the hospital while Dad was reading him psalms. Two days later I had flown to Illinois for the funeral.

I knew my grandpa. He always carried a pitch pipe in his pocket and never missed an opportunity to sing a barbershop tune. He wore overalls smeared with grease and paint, and I never knew he was telling one of his jokes until the punch line. He was a big man. I like to think he needed that large body to hold all his personality, both gruff and jolly.

I flew to Illinois to say goodbye to my grandpa, but mostly to be with my dad. He's one of my closest friends, and I wanted to be with him for a few days. Both of his parents were gone now, and being the oldest in the family, he was responsible for closing the books on Grandpa's life—paying and canceling bills, cleaning out his house and selling it, writing thank you cards, and saying goodbyes to the people and places he would no longer have any reason to visit. My mom needed to be back at work the day after the funeral, so I was his companion for the week.

The first few days I felt guilty for not missing April and Alleke. Did it make me a bad person that I didn't really miss being a dad or a husband while I was gone? Then one morning I was sitting in my dad's truck in front of the bank while he ran in to run an errand, and I picked up his Bible off the seat, unzipped the leather cover, and found this poem:

> There is a time for everything,
>> and a season for every activity under heaven:

a time to be born and a time to die,
a time to plant and a time to uproot,
a time to kill and a time to heal,
a time to tear down and a time to build,
a time to weep and a time to laugh,
a time to mourn and a time to dance,
a time to scatter stones and a time to gather them,
a time to embrace and a time to refrain,
a time to search and a time to give up,
a time to keep and a time to throw away,
a time to tear and a time to mend,
a time to be silent and a time to speak,
a time to love and a time to hate,
a time for war and a time for peace.

I did miss April and Alleke. I just didn't want to be with them. My priorities had temporarily shifted, and my dad needed me. I was where I needed to be at the time.

Death puts things into perspective. It reminds us that we all have an expiration date, and we might as well put ourselves to good use while we're still around. I kept thinking that I hoped Alleke would do the same for me someday. I hoped she would come and take care of me when my parents passed on. I hoped she would be willing to be my daughter when I needed her to be my daughter, even if she was already a mother too and that was more important most of the time.

1 YEAR, 11 MONTHS, 19 DAYS

Dumpster Diving

Today after I put Alleke down for a nap, I began clearing the dishes from lunch, which included eating the cold eggplant parmesan off Alleke's plate and checking to see if she had left any chocolate milk in her glass.

What most people don't realize is that cleaning up after a toddler is a completely legitimate form of dumpster diving. I was delighted to discover the hunk of dark chocolate floating in Alleke's glass, and after thinking to myself, *It's not a great job perk, but I'll take it*, I finished off the glass of milk.

I nibbled on the chocolate chunk as I carried the plates to the kitchen, but when the chunk didn't melt away, but got chewy like gum instead, I began to wonder what other food had been on Alleke's plate that she might have dropped in her glass when April and I weren't looking.

After setting the dishes down on the counter, I spit the chunk back into the cup and looked inside. Instead of finding a chewed-up grape seed, which was my guess, I found a smashed fly with only one wing left.

1 YEAR, 11 MONTHS, 21 DAYS
Wednesdays

I dropped a wrench on Alleke's foot this morning. I told her to stay away while I was pulling the toolbox out of the cupboard, but she ran up to see what I was doing anyway. The wrench fell out of the box and split open her big toe.

My gut reaction was to call April to find out what to do, but it was Wednesday morning, and I take care of Alleke on Wednesday mornings specifically so that April can go to a café and have some time for herself.

Wednesday mornings are the one time in the week that I can't ask for help. I have to parent all by myself. The experience is like being stranded on a deserted island with a toddler. I have to be resourceful. Even if I don't know how to do something—say, for

example if I don't know whether my child's toe is broken or if
it's serious enough that I should figure out which medical clinics
are covered by our insurance and which one is the closest of the
bunch—well, then, I have to figure it out, or nothing gets done.

It's easy for me to think I'm an involved parent until I get
to Wednesday morning and realize I don't know what Alleke
normally eats for breakfast or which key April uses to get on
the roof to hang up diapers or where we keep our Band-aids.

As a result, I watch April more closely the rest of the week
because I know Wednesday is coming.

Wednesday mornings aren't only about me being a competent
parent, but they're also about building a trusting relationship
with Alleke. We were at my parents' house a few months ago,
and Alleke tumbled down some stairs. I went running, but my
mom was already there. Usually my mom lets us call the shots
when it comes to our kids. She learned how to be a grandma
from her first two kids. This time, however, she said, "I got
her" and picked up Alleke. She rocked Alleke in her arms until
Alleke quieted down, then explained that unless she was able to
comfort Alleke when she needed to be comforted, Alleke would
never learn to trust her. Alleke wouldn't know from experience
that her grandma could be trusted to help her if she got hurt
or needed help with something.

When Alleke gets hurt, she always runs to Mom. Even when
I pick her up, she cries until I hand her to Mom. Except on
Wednesday mornings, when I'm her only option–then she lets
me comfort her.

I might not be her first choice, but she still trusts me, which
is a good reminder for both of us.

So, after the wrench fell on Alleke's toe, she sat on my lap
with her blankie. When she felt brave enough, she ventured off
and hopped around the house the rest of the morning—her toe
a fat blueberry.

1 YEAR, 11 MONTHS, 22 DAYS
Amsterdam

Who knew it would be so difficult to send my wife away to Amsterdam for a couple days to herself? Especially when April loves to travel, Amsterdam is one of her favorite cities, and I offered to keep Alleke at home with me while April was gone.

The idea was to send April to Amsterdam for a weekend conference while Alleke and I stayed in Madrid. April often says, "It's been two years since I've slept more than five hours in a row," which is true, because Alleke still wakes up often during the night, and April has only been away from Alleke once for more than 18 hours. So, I suggested that April take an extra day in Amsterdam to do whatever she wanted to—to go nuts and to enjoy her independence. After three days of intense negotiations, however, I was happy that at least she decided to go to Amsterdam, although she still took a couple days to muster the courage to actually buy her plane ticket.

What's most interesting to me is not that April resisted the idea to go to Amsterdam for the weekend. April is a good mom. She has done what most moms do if they have the chance, which is to give her child what she has needed most in her first two years of life: someone Alleke could trust to be there for her and whom she could rely on to meet her needs. What's more basic and reasonable than a mother's desire to protect her young?

What I find the most interesting is how hard I tried to convince April to leave, so I could be a single dad for a couple days.

Why? It's called liminality. Anthropologist Victor Turner used the term in his studies of various rites of passage among African people groups. In some tribes young boys were cared for by their mothers until they reached initiation age, which was around 13 years old. At that point the men would kidnap the boys, blindfold them, rough them up, circumcise them, and leave them in the bush to fend for themselves, sometimes up to six months. Once a month the tribal elders would go to meet the boys to give them guidance, but overall, they had to find both the inner and outer resources to survive, which involved learning to trust each other and work well together. Their relationships were forged out of this ordeal.

Liminality, then, describes a rite of passage, a change in relationship as a result of going through a challenging experience together. (I read about this in a book called *The Forgotten Ways* by Alan Hirsch.)

When April is around, Alleke and I rely on her. April holds us together as a family. Still, I yearn for the kind of experience where Alleke and I can prove that we trust each other, independent of anyone else. Not just in theory, but in practice. The only way to do this is to put ourselves in a situation where we have to rely on each other, where we have no other choice.

So, after April gets on a plane for Amsterdam early Thursday morning, Alleke and I will have exactly four days to find out if we trust each other. Hopefully we can survive without begging our "tribal elder" to come home.

1 YEAR, 11 MONTHS, 26 DAYS
Casserole

I helped Alleke pull on her stocking cap and tied it under her chin, then lifted her into my arms and took one more look around the apartment before we would catch the metro and surprise April at the airport.

The toys were put away. The floors were mopped. The laundry was folded in neat stacks on the couch. The table was set for three with a warm casserole in the oven. A pan of muffins was waiting on the counter for the following morning. Alleke and I had survived—all four days, all 96 hours, all 5,760 minutes, and it was a cause for celebration. As a result, I had spent the day getting the house ready for April's return.

Still, as I stood at the front door and looked around the apartment at my handiwork, I suddenly wished I had spent the day differently. Alleke and I had finished a marathon week of dinners with friends—five nights in a row. Today was the day I had set aside for Alleke and me, but I had spent it getting the house ready for April to return.

Left to parent Alleke by myself, I could see more clearly how my parenting style was distinct from April's, which included my endless compulsion to get things done.

I set goals. I make lists. I do things. I'm an achiever to the very core of my being, but as I thought back through the day, it became painfully clear to me that doing one more thing for someone is not always enough.

At one point during the afternoon while I was making the casserole Alleke woke up from her nap. I didn't have time to stop and cuddle with her like April usually does because I had a pot boiling on the stove, so I put her in the baby carrier on my front and let her snuggle up against my chest while I cut up vegetables and listened to NPR. Alleke was trying to tell me a story, and I guess I wasn't listening well or at least not looking at her because eventually she took my head in her hands and turned it to face her, so she had my attention. She said she wanted to get down, and she wanted a snack. I unclipped the baby carrier, let her down, and handed her an apple.

"Go nuts," I said, hoping she would wander into the living room to eat her apple so I could keep cooking. Instead, Alleke reached for my hand and pulled me into the living room. She demanded that I close the kitchen door behind me, and she pointed at the couch.

"Sit," she said. I sat down and waited while she disappeared in her room and returned with a stack of books, which she set on my lap before climbing on the couch and taking a bite of her apple.

"Read books," she said, coaching me step-by-step through this simple exercise in quality time.

I think I read maybe one book before making some excuse about having to stir the veggies boiling on the stove.

I regret cooking and baking and mopping and tidying and folding clothes instead of reading books or blowing bubbles or playing with finger paints or going for a bike ride. Alleke wanted some attention, but I chose to get things done instead.

We surprised April at the airport and talked all the way home. By the time we arrived at the apartment, and after much giggling and cuddling and a quick game of hide-and-go-seek, it was late. Much too late for a casserole dinner.

1 YEAR, 11 MONTHS, 27 DAYS

Reference Point

I watched Alleke take two clementines from the bowl and set them down on the table in front of her. She looked at them for a while, as if these two ordinary clementines might unlock some key to the universe, then pointed at the bigger one and said "Daddy" and at the smaller one and said "Alleke."

Lately, Alleke has been arranging things this way, in pairs. The big one is always daddy, and the small one is always Alleke. The first time, while we were watching *Finding Nemo,* she chased the fish around the screen with her finger and labeled Marlin as "Daddy" and Nemo as "Alleke." Then it was the lions at the zoo, next our pet goldfish, and eventually measuring cups, shoes, water bottles, even popcorn kernels. It's always the same: I'm big. She's small.

What's the meaning of all this? At the very least, Alleke knows the difference between big and small. She's learned to compare.

Perhaps the greater significance is that I'm a reference point, a standard in Alleke's life, and in one way or another she will always measure the universe according to me.

I am the yardstick Alleke uses to figure out what a man looks like, and a husband, and a father, and while I can't promise to be the perfect man—although I do my best—I can promise to be the man in her life for a while and to share with her what I know, so that when the time comes, she'll know a good man when she sees him.

1 YEAR, 11 MONTHS, 28 DAYS
The Moon

From the couch, I could see the moon. It was a strange thing to see the moon caught there between the window frame and the roofline in the middle of the afternoon.

Alleke climbed up on the couch next to me. I pointed, and she saw the moon too. We sat there side-by-side with our heads back, like we were in dentist chairs, and looked up at the white dot in the sky.

Later, when Alleke was in footie pajamas, and we sat reading stories in the rocking chair in her bedroom, she wanted to read the blue book with the moon on the front of it. She pointed at the moon on every page. I found another book with a moon in it, and she pointed at the moon in that book too, each time looking up at me to make sure I saw it as well.

There it was, the moon.

Over the course of the next few days while I carried Alleke around the city on my back, I would catch her leaning way back in the baby carrier looking for the moon, and sometimes she would find it.

I wondered if Alleke's obsession with the moon had to do with the simple fact that the moon always came back. If she kept looking, eventually she would find it again. For now, the moon was her Jesus. The moon was one of the few things in her life, besides her mom and dad, that was usually the same and usually there. The moon was a reference point for her.

I grew up on the rim of the horizon, on a small acreage on a gravel road in Iowa. There were many things that never changed, like the sky over me and the dirt under my feet.

Alleke, on the other hand, is growing up in the city, a place that reinvents itself constantly. Nothing seems certain or eternal. One building goes up, another comes down. Friendships come and go, jobs change, and we move around. We filter out strangers and street noise and try to ground ourselves somewhere, being intentional about seeing the same people and going the same places, because it doesn't happen naturally—not here.

Maybe that's why when Alleke is looking for something she knows, she looks up.

In a few months Alleke will go to preschool, and once again, everything will change for her—everything, that is, except for her mom, her dad, and the moon.

The story continues at becomingdadbook.com...

INDEX

ABOUT THE AUTHOR

Kelly Crull is the author of a children's book, *Clara Has a Baby Brother*, and a parenting blog, spaindad.com, which was one of Google's top-ranked "baby blogs," syndicated by a number of online dad networks and featured as a link at Glamour.com. He has been featured as a new voice in parenting in various La Leche League newsletters, *The Father Life* magazine, AttachmentParenting.com and DIYFather.com. His parenting videos have appeared on *Good Morning America*, *The Today Show*, Slate.com, Marca.com and have received YouTube's "Top 50 Videos of the Week" award.

Kelly is originally from Iowa. He lives with his wife and two children in Madrid, Spain.

Printed in Great Britain
by Amazon

77550901R00144